DIVA DECISIONS

DIVA DECISIONS

*How to Get From Smart to Intelligent
By Claiming Your Power of Choice*

Dr. V. Brooks Dunbar, D.M.
Life & Leadership Coach

Diva Decisions: How to Get from Smart to Intelligent by Claiming Your Power of Choice
© 2017 by Dr. V. Brooks Dunbar

All Rights Reserved
Printed in the United States

This book or parts thereof may not be reproduced in whole or in part, in any form or by any means, stored in any retrieval system, or transmitted in any form by any means—electronic, mechanical, photocopying, recording, or by any other information storage and retrieval system now known or hereafter invented—without prior written permission from the publisher, except as provided by United States of America copyright law. For permission requests, write to the publisher, at "Attention: Book Permissions," at the address below.

Library of Congress Control Number: 2017942691
ISBN: 978-0-9987966-0-4
Published by The Center for Confidence, LLC, Jacksonville Florida 32207
First Edition
Book Cover & Design: Nuance Art, LLC
via www.aCreativeNuance.com

Mail the publisher at:
The Center for Confidence, LLC
841 Prudential Dr., 12th Floor
Jacksonville, Florida 32207
www.thecenterforconfidence.com
info@thecenterforconfidence.com
www.facebook.com/thecenterforconfidence

This book may be ordered by mail from the publisher. For information about special discounts available for bulk purchases, sales promotions, fundraising and educational needs, contact The Center for Confidence, LLC, ATT: Book Sales at 1-904-372-1942 or info@thecenterforconfidence.com

DEDICATION

To Lauretta, Lucille and all the women in my family.
And, my other moms Ms. Cassandra and Ms. Donna.
And, with much love for Grandma Irene and Grandma Hazel.
To my husband, SMSgt Kenneth Roy Dunbar Jr.
aka "Chip."

CONTENTS

DEDICATION I
INTRODUCTION 1
SELF 12
    1. Getting to Intelligent *14*
    2. IQ, EQ, and EI are Relative *34*
    3. Never, Never, Relinquish Your Power *46*
    4. Question Authority *73*
    5. Make Peace With Your Sexuality *90*
    6. Find Your Authentic Self *106*
CAREER **129**
    7. Own Your Persona, Manage It Well *130*
    8. Yes, Pretty is a Talent… Use it Wisely *158*
    9. Trust but verify *172*
    10. Create Multiple Versions of Yourself *182*
RELATIONSHIPS **192**
    11. Practice Self-Preservation Daily *193*
    12. Know Your Price and Worth *209*
    13. Adapt and Overcome *225*
    14. Eliminate Judgment *233*
    15. Get a Reality Check *252*

PERSONAL SPACE **266**
- *16. Love is Not a Guarantee 267*
- *17. Bet on Fear 281*
- *18. Get a Personal Coach 288*
- *19. Inspiration 308*

CONCLUSION **319**
LAST WORDS **322**
ABOUT THE AUTHOR **324**
THE CENTER FOR CONFIDENCE **326**
ACKNOWLEDGMENTS **329**
LIST OF TABLES, DIAGRAMS AND CHARTS **330**
LIST OF HASHTAGS **331**
READER'S RESOURCES **332**
REFERENCES **337**

DIVA
DECISIONS

"If I had any talent in the world, any talent that God could give me, I would be a great diva."

— *Ruth Bader Ginsburg, aka "The Notorious RBG"*

INTRODUCTION

To be smart is to know, to be intelligent is to understand.

Diva Decisions is written for creative career women who want confidence and the skills to make more intelligent decisions. A creative career woman is a talented self-starter who is workforce ready or entering her second or third career. She is multi-talented and may work multiple jobs, while taking care of her family. She is a diva by definition as a woman of extraordinary talent, drive and an inherent and divine power to lead and succeed. She is smart, successful and goal oriented, but unfortunately, she has yet to fully appreciate the capacity of her power of choice to be fully who she chooses to be.

Over the last few decades I've worked in Corporate America and as a mentor and life coach for young women new to the workforce and professional women already established in their career. During this time I've noticed a pattern of thoughts and ensuing behaviors that hinder our progression to knowledge and true intelligence. I don't mean the type of intelligence that comes from books and education. I mean the type of intelligence that can be only be acquired by self-exploration and self-awareness through our life experiences. When we become truly intelligent we start to think for ourselves, based on our past, present and where we see ourselves in the future.

What made me come to this belief is the sharp contrast to where I am now as a woman who has traveled across multiple continents, lived and worked internationally, and dared to succeed on my own merits and talent as an entrepreneur and businesswoman. Yet nearly three decades ago I, like my parents, had never traveled by plane, my palate was limited to American food or Chinese takeout, and my relationships were uncomplicated, unchallenging, and predictable. I was rarely out of my comfort zone. Most of my life experiences had taken place in the state where I was born and went to college. I asked for little from life and I gave as much in return.

I had never given serious thought to expanding my life experiences or delving deep into who I was and why I was making those choices in my life. I had never thought of all the opportunities open to me or that I could learn from them for self-empowerment and to expand my world view. Perhaps I was caught up with doing things with my friends and family. Or maybe I was distracted by the demands of school or work. Or could it simply be a matter of my own way of thinking? Perhaps I thought I was already self-aware and that the choices and decisions I'd made—in part because of the people around me—were already taking me where I needed to go. But that was not the case. By relying on other people's idea of what I was capable of, I had boxed myself in. Until I learned to think for myself, I would never understand how my life could drastically change for the better. Or how I could understand my thought process and subsequently change my life.

Understanding our life experiences starts with the ability (or inability) to learn across the four dimensions of our life and the mental capacity to think deeply and often as if it were a daily exercise. I refer to these four dimensions as the LifeSpace, which represents our self, career, relationships and personal space; or the 4D LifeSpace. It is dynamic and fluid. This space allows us to be self-transforming as we constantly adapt to the ongoing changes in our environment and life.

The term LifeSpace is not a new one. It is borrowed from my time at the U.S. Army Medical Command when then Army Surgeon General, Lt. Gen. Patricia

Horoho,[i] introduced it as the signature program of her four-year tenure. Horoho who was the Army's first female surgeon general and first nurse to hold the position, rose to prominence during the September 11 attacks on the Pentagon and was recognized for bravery when she coordinated and rendered first aid to victims.

Because Horoho was a woman and a nurse, her appointment was not well received by some. This was because not only was she a woman, but she was the first nurse in a position traditionally held by physicians. Regardless, her authority and power came to be respected by all because she was exceptional.

The result was a refocus on treating health and promoting wellness through prevention by improving sleep, activity and nutrition within the LifeSpace. There was also a shift to put the onus on the patient to take responsibility for his or her own care when outside of the doctor's office, which would aid in prevention. *Diva Decisions* views self-care from the four dimensions of the human experience—self, career, relationships and personal space. They feed our physical and emotional growth and development.

Horoho was succeeded by Lt. Gen. Nadya West, the current Army surgeon general and first American of

African descent to hold the position. You and I, like Horoho, feel a sense of urgency to make a difference in our lives. *Diva Decisions* cuts through the blind spots in our thinking, the outdated models of womanhood, and gives new context to the meaning of contemporary woman. The book is filled with personal stories offered by women, like you and I, mothers, daughters, professional women, and young women just starting out, who have experienced breakthrough moments that changed the trajectory of their lives. I balance their stories with practical advice on how you can use their experiences to address the areas of your life that can use positive change. I then give you the tools to make those changes.

In the book I discuss how to question authority and why you *should* question authority. I detail why you should never relinquish your power and how we often give up our power without even knowing it. We also talk about making peace with our sexuality and finding our authentic self. We then explore how you can create multiple versions of yourself to adapt to the changes in your environment and relationships in the workplace and at home. Along the way we work on eliminating judgment, of ourself and others, to grow on a personal, financial and emotional level.

Smart is knowing how to think and apply knowledge or skills to accomplish tasks. Intelligence is knowing how to think and also *understand* across changing situations or social, political, and cultural environments that require technical skill, social awareness, and emotional management. Smart is relying more on talent or skill. Intelligence demands a high level of *awareness* of skills, the *meaning* of relationships between people and things, and *management* of emotional energy coming from yourself and from others. To be smart is to have limited awareness and a narrow focus. To be intelligent is to see broadly and creatively while understanding that learning is a continuum that requires a high level of awareness of ourself and others. Learning will never stop long enough for us to be all wise and all knowing. Therefore, intelligence is to apply the correct balance of knowledge to the appropriate situation and the parameters of the environment, at the right time.

Diva Decisions is organized into four sections that represent the LifeSpace. Each section has personal stories of breakthrough moments that led to more intelligent thinking and behavior. Each chapter concludes with tips or action steps that can be immediately incorporated into your life. For example, Chapter 1, *Getting to Intelligent*, summarizes the key points of the chapter "What is Your Choice?" and follows with "Six Tips for Critical Thinking" to help make informed decisions. One of these tips is to practice mindfulness, which will increase self-awareness of the positive or negative energy you may be unconsciously sending out.

I also give you tips on managing love and loss, and discuss why it is important to trust but also why it is equally important to verify that trust. We talk about how to overcome the fear of new experiences and why fear is important to growth. Throughout, we discuss the importance of finding inspiration through leaders, influencers and decision makers, and whether or not a life coach is for you. Some chapters also include a workbook section with tables to chart your responses and feedback to visually see how and where you can improve in specific areas.

My goal with writing *Diva Decisions* is to help you get from smart to intelligent. The stories you'll read show how many women, in all walks of life—many of them like you and I—have gotten from smart to intelligent. For me, it was the moment I realized that the saying "Hard work pays off" was simply not true, nor will our hard work ever really pay off without the social and emotional awareness associated with intelligence. That aha moment came a few days after I was passed over for yet another promotion. But it didn't end there, I had also lost the bid for the president of my professional association. I was instead offered the role of secretary.

I knew then that I had mastered the skills and competencies to accomplish tasks and meet goals. But, I had missed the opportunity to learn how to lead and succeed. That would come through understanding how to influence and motivate people, which required intelligence. The third thing I learned was that I was waiting for answers, meanwhile to get them required me to take actions and make hard choices. Ultimately I learned that my employers weren't responsible for championing my professional development; I was. Once I learned that these decisions were mine to make, I could go about making them.

In *Diva Decisions,* the journey to intelligent comes from the personal stories of women I've coached, mentored, and managed in the workplace. They include past coworkers and clients, friends and family members. I also use news articles that resonated with the themes and challenges experienced by other inspiring and passionate women. These trailblazers are making a path, sometimes unknowingly, for us to follow that allows us to live more intelligent lives. These stories are fiction, though based on fact. The names and places have been changed and some of the specifics and elements have been enhanced for contrast and clarity, but the message and the lessons they've learned are intact. They will help guide you along your journey as you learn about theirs. Their journey and lessons answer the most important question: "What does every woman need to not only survive but to also thrive, intellectually, spiritually, and emotionally?" The answer is, and appears to have always been, intelligence—in its many degrees of expression and application for decision making, problem solving, and creative thinking in the present moment and the future.

Getting to intelligent is also about safety and protecting ourselves from customs, traditions, beliefs and values that bind us to unhealthy cycles of behavior. But more than anything else, it is about self-confidence and self–awareness. One of those dominant self-defeating behaviors is the tendency to position ourself as followers, not as leaders. When my association appointed me to the role of secretary rather than elect me as president, I declined. At that moment, I made a choice to disrupt the task and goal-oriented behavior that fed into this perception of me as a task manager who excelled at moving and managing *things*, not *people*.

The principles I outline in *Diva Decisions* create a woman's survival guide for how to thrive at work, at home and out in the world. As the Founder and Lead Coach at The Center for Confidence, in Jacksonville, Florida, I offer strategies to improve how people as well as organizations function. Through life and leadership coaching I've met with men and women who are going through personal and career changes. I have been blessed to be allowed into their lives to help them move to the next level in their careers, and personal and interpersonal relationships. As I worked with them I realized that their stories, although unique to them, were also universal. I wanted to share not only their personal voyage to intelligent but also because I knew their experiences could help others.

I wrote *Diva Decisions* to empower you to engage and live fearlessly in the moments that make up the 365, 24/7 cycle of our hectic modern day lives. In it are stories of the many women who have achieved balance and insight—in their careers, love life, and family relationships—by using the lens of self-awareness and reflection.

These are the stories of how we can get from smart to intelligent. It follows a simple mantra: To be smart is to know, to be intelligent is to understand.

Self

"The beginning of wisdom is the definition of terms."
— Socrates

Noun: Self is a person's essential being that distinguishes them from others, especially considered as the object of introspection or reflexive action.

Synonyms: ego, I, oneself, persona, person, identity, character, personality, psyche, soul, spirit, mind, (inner) being.

Self is our individuality, our personal truth and identity, and our level of consciousness for how we fit into the world around us. It is encompassing of our ability to self-manage. It challenges the old saying that "we are all the same." We are emotionally different from the day we were born into our particular situation with our particular personality and developmental traits. Self-confidence, allows us to access and acknowledge your own power to breed success.

1
GETTING TO INTELLIGENT

"I'm attracted to intelligence, not education. You could graduate from the best, most elite college, but if you're still clueless about the world and society, you don't know anything." — *Unknown*

This my story. My journey to intelligent started when I was seventeen and I had a powerful conversation with Coach Dailey, my high school gym coach. I was a tall, skinny kid from a rural town outside of Ocala, Florida thirty minutes from my alma mater, the University of Florida. It ends with me as a twenty-nine-year-old graduate student studying human resources at Florida International University in Miami. This story is important because it illustrates my journey to get from smart to intelligent by thinking and understanding, beyond learning and knowing information. And it all started with this conversation.

BROOKS

Looking back, I can say with the utmost confidence that although I graduated from high school with a 4.2 grade point average, I was unintelligent even with a full semester of college credits already under my belt. Looking forward, I can say with the same amount of confidence that my fifteen nieces and nephews, cousins, and stepdaughters, are graduating from high school and college with the same level of intelligence, which is minimal at best. This is the usual outcome despite all of the technology and new media available in our tightly connected global and social world in which we live.

In school, my teachers told me I was smart, assigned me to special projects, and assured me that I would be successful one day. They nurtured me with the care of a parent whose words of encouragement would get me through my insecurities and self doubt. At home my parents added more praise after seeing my grades and performance reports. These positive responses taught me to keep doing what I was doing. I was a robot responding to stimulation that came from repeating the same pattern—study hard—break for interim report—study hard—break for mid-term report—study hard—break for final report—repeat.

No one ever *asked* why or for what purpose I was excelling at academic activities. They *told* me instead, that it was so I could ultimately get a good job and be a productive citizen and that this was the only way I could do it. So there it was, if I studied, and memorized everything I needed to do well on tests, it would make me smart. The end result was a guarantee that I would be successful. Everything would come to me: wealth, fulfillment, financial security, happiness, wellbeing. I was certain they were correct, and with my high school experience almost behind me, I pre-registered to attend summer courses at the University of Florida.

It was Coach Dailey, who, completely by accident, opened my eyes and made me aware that this simple routine of getting good grades in exchange for adult affirmation, wasn't necessarily the path to self-awareness, self-exploration, self-fulfillment, or even financial security in a job I loved.

On the day I had this breakthrough, it was a typical swelteringly hot afternoon in Florida. I was standing in the senior parking lot during lunch break waiting for my sister to deliver my class project. Although the assignment was due before class, my teacher okayed me to turn it in before the end of the school day. She had extended an olive branch, but we both knew the only time to receive the project before the day ended was during my lunch hour. Hours later, I was standing there alone, sweating in a hot parking lot. Seeing me, Coach Dailey walked over and asked why I was there. I explained my situation and when I finished he said, "Why don't you have your sister take it to the administration office where they can receive it for you and you can pick it up when you're dismissed from class?"

This simple solution caught me off guard and I wondered, Why hadn't I thought of that? I wouldn't have to wait in the sweltering heat and maybe damage my project as I lugged it from class to class.

That was when I realized that my reflexive behavior was actually limiting. Coach pointed out that there was a different and more intelligent way to accomplish a very simple task. For years, I had been primed to do exactly as I was told and in the way I was told to do it. Coach Dailey made me aware that I could do it another way, a way that would be more beneficial to me. Ultimately, he made me aware that I could think for myself. It was a brief encounter between the grasshopper and the teacher, but Coach Dailey wasn't finished.

"You have a lot of book sense, but no common sense." He finished, then he was off to the gym. His words startled me and have stuck with me ever since.

I thought a lot about our exchange. I wondered how I could have overlooked something so seemingly simple and straightforward. It got me thinking that perhaps I was not as smart as everyone had led me to believe. Perhaps I wasn't even smart enough to go to college. What had I missed in all those years of primary and secondary education, including passing advanced placement courses and completing college prep programs? When I presented these questions to my older brother, who was by far not the smartest in the family, he agreed with coach.

"You're all books and brains, but no bravado." He said in his usual matter-of-fact way.

Even though his words annoyed me, I knew exactly what he meant. I didn't have the guts to question or challenge anything. I simply went along with the status quo without deviation.

Why had he not told me this before? I wondered.

Prior to this—I have to call it an awakening—my self-confidence, or what I believed to be self-confidence, was indisputable. It had been created, built up and measured by my role models. These were my parents, teachers, professors, community leaders, friends and acquaintances, who patterned the way I socialized and behaved. Although well meaning, it wasn't a true depiction of me. It was really a reflection of them, of their role and positive contribution to my development. In response, their praise made me feel confident in my ability to do anything. Teachers wanted to feel that their time had value. Parents wanted to feel their kids' accomplishments were a reflection of them. Not only had I been duped into being a "good soldier" but my brother had known it all along.

How did this caring coach help me to get closer to intelligent with only a few words, when caring teachers and parents had failed? It's simple. He started me on the road to thinking for myself.

Of course, thinking about things was something I already thought I was good at. But as I thought back on what coach's observation and instruction really meant, it became clear that I was a follower. And as a follower, I had become naturally oriented to behaviors that required thinking only to the extent that it provided a response to a direct request. As a smart student, my obligation was to complete my homework as asked, study as expected (asking was no longer required), and attend courses on time. However, these were the routines and thought processes expected of children, not for young adults.

I now understand that in academic environments, whether it's a secondary or post-secondary setting, athletic coaches, by far, appear to be the few educators who see things in context and feel more empowered to set you straight. It even seemed they would bend the rules if needed, to get you back on track.

We have seen numerous examples of coaches stepping in to bring out the best in students and adults. The stories professional athletes tell of their journey is remarkable when told through the narrative of a caring coach. These accounts of how impoverished, shy and bullied kids had a strong coach to help them, on and off the playing field, are the subject of movies, documentaries, memoirs, and self-help books. They have convinced me, that everyone needs an effective coach, whether it's a personal coach, life coach, business coach, or leadership coach.

Today, I see the same lack of awareness I had, in my nieces, cousins, and stepdaughters who represent pre-workforce, workforce ready, and collegiate age groups. They have book smarts but not necessarily common sense. The independent free thinkers—who have more common sense than book smarts—have the opportunity to be more successful than their book smart rivals.

Regardless, we all share a common shortcoming; we are all unaware of our potential, and our range of intelligence. So what went wrong?

> *"Whatever the cost of our libraries, the price is cheap compared to an ignorant nation."* — Walter Cronkite

I found the answer to that question through years of experience and career development where, my common-sense decision making was constantly tested in the sometimes artificial but necessary relationships of the workplace. That was where career success depended on my ability to work effectively with people from different cultures, backgrounds, nationalities, and ethnicities, who had diverse behaviors, perspectives and opinions. My work in the nonprofit sector as a research and proposal writer gave me insight into the challenges of senior citizens, the poor, and at-risk children and youth. When I transitioned into the private sector as a disaster responder for an insurance company, my experience with corporate culture and the relationship with government brought an awareness of the competitiveness and fast pace of the corporate sector in contrast to the slow bureaucracy of the private sector, as well as the benefits of each.

The corporate sector was free to implement current training and professional development while individuals in the public sector seemed to be ten years behind current leadership and management policy. I later realized this depended on the prioritization agencies received when it came to the allocation of public resources. My work as a fundraiser, professor and researcher in higher education introduced me to the competitiveness of academia and how education initiatives are delivered or defunded when administrators are left to decide on the hierarchy of programs in need of funding. It also enlightened me to the complex relationships between administrators, students, and academics that required careful balancing between politics, sports, and college culture. As an entrepreneur, I learned to work with small micro enterprises, corporations and professional associations.

As a female a business owner, entrepreneur and executive, it became clear that gender and sexuality were ongoing challenges, which when managed well, made the difference between success and failure. I've also traveled as a military spouse, international scholar and cultural tourist, which all required me to be adaptable and proactive as well as appropriately reactive.

My diverse personal and academic experiences have positioned me in a LifeSpace that few experience, and has shown me not only what I am good at but also what I like doing the most. I like helping people. After working in the nonprofit sector, I thought I understood the best and not so best in people even when they are driven by a common passion to help others. When I worked for academia, I thought I had a firm grasp of organizational behaviors, but I soon learned that an organizational culture, like higher education, brought with it a tendency to be laissez-faire and at times elitist. In these envirnoments many faculty members are tenured. This meant lifetime employment without any possibility of removal except under rare circumstances, regardless of their teaching impact or value to their students' broader learning.

Working in a military environment also changed my perspective. I questioned the practical usefulness of intelligence as a necessary ingredient for the acquisition of power and authority. In particular, when the lives of very young and passionate men and women were placed in the hands of leaders whose comparative range of intelligent was not at the level needed to help them lead responsibly or intelligently. These task-oriented leaders saw people as things to be managed. They directed and ordered them around with the same compassion and regard given to the use of a tool, and not the interaction with a human being.

My curiosity and my desire to strengthen my common-sense skills led me to be curious about people, and the way we think things through and why. My sense of urgency has reached a peak as educational institutions are becoming more and more technology-based and remote. The numbers of pre-college graduates are increasing and opportunities for a personal and caring coach to unapologetically interject are shrinking because of it. Subsequently we may have to get to intelligent on our own. The stories in *Diva Decisions* will help you do that.

Intelligence is a leadership trait. I first learned of the presence of multiple intelligences and their relationship to leadership in my master's degree program. My academic research followed Bernard Bass, a leadership scholar who studied the relationship between leadership, cognition and intelligence.

The word cognition was new to me. However, it is the most important word I've never been taught. Cognition is how we think. Meta-cognition refers to how we *think* about *thinking*. Let cognition be a word you come to understand intimately. Just like walking and talking, cognition should signal a natural reflex about how to think. We know how to walk, fast, slow, in long stride, in short steps, with a skip or a rhythm depending on the situation. So too, should we know how to think, fast or slow, which is most often associated with thinking in crisis or normal environments. We also think in patterns, which is most often associated with intuitive thought, in abstract or concrete thoughts. Lastly, we also think deeply or introspectively depending on the situation. When we begin to acknowledge how we think and what works or doesn't work, we will start to achieve the desired outcomes for specific situations.

Bass defines cognitive intelligence as the *"verbal, spatial and numerical aptitude factors along with various aptitudes dealing with abstraction and complex problem solving, both fluid and concrete. Intellectual talents, skills, and achievements are also included."*[ii] In simpler terms, cognitive intelligence is our capacity to think through problems and in the correct context.

Bass's theory of multiple intelligences placed cognitive, social and emotional intelligence as the most important of numerous types of intelligence, including tacit intelligence and mechanical intelligence. Models of how leaders think generally reflect two approaches, as an activity of how leaders think in general, or through a more specific approach of how leaders think about specific types of issues or problems.[iii]

What I have discovered, is that researchers have known all along that there are a range of intelligences we all need to be successful. What is even more surprising is that these ranges of intelligences can be developed. The concept of developing my latent thinking skills to a level of critical thinking was a powerful opportunity and an enlightening worldview. For me, a graduate student at the age of twenty-nine, the writing was on the wall. You reduce your chances of being successful in all areas of life—self, career, relationships and personal space—if you focus only on being smart.

For the six years I took to gain work experience after college, it appeared that experience alone had not been enough. My employers utilized me only to get the benefit of my technical competencies. The result in five years had been nominal promotions and salary increases as expected. It was clear to me that moving up in the company was not in my future. What was in store for me was to progress or matriculate. However, I felt my calling was more than spending a lifetime matriculating through a company. Especially now that I knew the difference. I was smart because I had the technical skills and talent to perform the job. Unfortunately, I did not understand that effectiveness on the job required so much more than that. I had to get to intelligent.

Why are we not taught these critical skills at the earliest age possible? Currently, access to these teachable skills is largely concentrated in higher education programs that cost time, money and preparation. These factors make learning available to only a few who can afford it. The rest of us are denied what I consider the soft skills that should be the baseline of teaching and learning fundamentals and made available to everyone.

What is Your Choice?

Smart is knowing how to think and apply knowledge or skills to accomplish a task or meet a goal. Intelligence is knowing how to both think and understand across changing situations or social, political, and cultural environments. This requires the right professional or technical skills, social awareness, and emotional management. (#DIVAgetintelligent)

The first step for acquiring technical skills is more readily accessible through education and training. The next step is to improve your social intelligence. Social and emotional intelligence is the ability to be aware of our own emotions and those of others, in the moment, and to use that information to manage ourselves and manage our relationships. The importance of understanding how social context and emotions, influence our thinking and decisions will make a big difference in how successfully work, life, and play can be accomplished. Changing our LifeSpace is only part of the picture. We must also see ourselves through the mirror of other people's perspectives. We must then use that raw intelligence to inform our choices. If we do, the outcomes will be more successful.

Six Tips for Critical Thinking
(The Exercise from Where Informed Decisions Flow):

1. Practice mindfulness by being aware of your presence and the energy you project to the people and things around you.
2. Understand the dynamics in human personality and character. Observe how people tend to behave when alone and in groups, or under pressure.
3. Develop situational awareness to observe cultural, political, and social influences on the present environment and your ability to be successful across the LifeSpace.
4. Get to know people. Seek multiple perspectives from trusted confidants as well as intermittent acquaintances.
5. Find a confidante to test ideas.
6. Listen to all behavioral cues both verbal and non-verbal.

Dr. V. Brooks Dunbar, D.M.

THE THREE-SKILL APPROACH OF SUCCESS AND INTELLIGENCE

Mastering Technical, Human, and Conceptual Skills

Any one of us can be successful in life if we possess an above average range of intelligence. The Three-Skill Approach[iv] centers on the argument that anyone can be successful if they develop and master technical, human, and conceptual skills that correspond with intelligence. These skills can be developed in all of us and correspond to the ability to problem solve, understand and socially interact with people, and process information in a meaningful way.

Three-Skill Approach can be used as a leadership tool to help define the characteristics associated with intelligent thinking and behavior. A mastery of these skills results in performance outcomes that lead to confidence and competency.

Technical skills generally refer to hard skills that can be learned or taught such as in educational programs, through training, or gained through experience. Human skills are our individual personality traits, character and behaviors that we develop and apply to form relationships. Conceptual skills refer to the ability to create meaning out of abstract ideas and hypotheticals. It is the measure of our ability to draw inferences, conclusions and make judgments.[v]

KEY CONCEPTS ASSOCIATED WITH THE THREE-SKILL APPROACH		
Technical, Human, and Conceptual Skills* associated with intelligence	Intelligence Skills (competencies)	Results
INPUT (experience, training, learning, behavior)	**OUTPUT** (your mental work)	**OUTCOME** (your impact)
• Perceptual Processing (insight/awareness) • Information Processing • Reasoning • Creative or Divergent Thinking • Memory • Comprehension • Mental Organizing and Structuring • Motivation • Personality	• Problem Solving • Social Judgment • Knowledge	• Effectiveness • Performance
Modified from Source: Northouse, 2004 (*social intelligence, mechanical intelligence, etc. what are the different intelligences?)		

We are all born with a certain level of cognitive ability or cognition and this ability becomes more crystallized over time as knowledge is learned and retained. Cognition, or intelligence, is indicated by how individuals apply these three skills and effectively interact in different situations to achieve the results and outcomes they want.

2
IQ, EQ, AND EI ARE RELATIVE

"Knowing others is intelligence; knowing yourself is true wisdom. Mastering others is strength; mastering yourself is true power." — Lao-Tzu

We understand there is a difference between personality and character traits that affects our ability to act intelligently. But, is it that simple?

Intelligence is a complex characteristic to understand. It is a confusing phenomenon. Why are brilliant people not so smart in some areas? How does someone without any formal education become a successful businessperson or entrepreneur?

A 2015 article titled "Super-Intelligence" in *New York* magazine[vi] effectively explained this confusion between intellect and its relationship to success. The magazine interviewed a person self-described as an under-performer in high school, and polyamorous, and super-intelligent. This proven genius shared that he has an Intelligence Quotient (IQ) score of 169 and scored

175 out of 180 on the *Law School Admission Test* (LSAT), which he admits he took with a friend only as a gesture of moral support. Regardless of his test scores, he readily told *New York* readers, "I still have no common sense." He then explained that, "Having a high IQ doesn't mean you are going to be successful. It just means your brain works faster. It recognizes patterns. It draws conclusions quickly."[vii]

The good news is that although we possess ranges of intelligence across scales of intelligence, brilliance and genius; leadership ability needs only a "keen mind," which requires having "above average intelligence rather than genius."[viii]

Research shows that half of all IQ scores (50%) fall between 90 and 110. I'm not a psychologist; however, my experience working with people across positions and roles, as a department director, supervisor, project manager, team leader, mentor, and professional coach, has offered me a theory of the span of learning and knowledge. I've experienced many ranges of reasoning, which have become useful for assessing one's capacity to be effective in the workplace and the resources I need to support their professional development.

The unscientific scale involves the following: (1) Those who are limited in reasoning for one reason or another. (2) Those who have the capacity to reason but do not have the knowledge or information to do so. (3) Those who have the knowledge or information but are limited in their ability to process it. (4) Those, like the twenty-something me, who have the ability to process information but don't know how. (5) Intelligent people who have the ability to process information and are in the throes of learning and knowledge acquisition. (6) Those who are at the maximum scale of learning and have the capacity to be perceptive and reflective aided by experience. (7) People who are perceptive and reflective regardless of experience aids. (8) People who comprehend beyond a range that can be explained.

I simply categorize these ranges of reason within stages of needed learning or career development. These maturing stages of cognition range from dense or ignorant, to smart or intelligent, and brilliant or genius. All are meaningful to the workplace and require different levels of coaching, training and development depending on the individual's talents and motivations to develop the skills they need. The key is understanding that they can all be successful if given the opportunity.

In contrast to IQ, which measures general intelligence, EQ or the emotional quotient intends to measure emotional intelligence (EI). It refers to our ability to understand ourself and others. Interpersonal and intrapersonal intelligence factors, reflect our ability to sense, understand, and effectively apply the acumen of emotions to manage these forms of human relations. There are many examples that illustrate the difference between IQ and EQ. For instance, Steve Jobs, co-founder of Apple, Inc. and regarded as the pioneer of the personal computer, is inarguably a genius with a very high IQ but he also had a very low EQ. He is depicted as an emotionally abusive narcissist in regard to his personal relationships and how he interacted with others.

If intelligence can be developed and skills associated with success can be learned, then why not start earlier than later? Some of the key factors of social intelligence cannot be learned, but must be experienced. If you are a self-starter, workforce ready or pre-college bound, this book will not focus on the technical skills our colleges and universities do a great job of teaching. Instead it concentrates on self-development of the two remaining skills associated with success and intelligence, these are the human and conceptual skills that must be understood and experienced for self-awareness of ourself and others. It is the development of these skills that reflect the presence of a higher order of intelligence.

This is where I will focus on the human side of intelligence and the skills to develop our full capacity for success. Look to the stories and lessons in this book to identify thought processes and the emergence of insight and intelligence, to see which thought processes and experiences more closely match your own. They will enlighten and prepare you to use the knowledge to make necessary changes.

Fortunately, today, many of us have a choice. However, many geniuses of the past did not. Albert Einstein, a late starter, was sent to a remedial school where he was allowed to express his creativity and only then did he begin to thrive. Nikola Tesla, was an electrical engineer and inventor who lived from 1856–1943. He developed the first alternating-current induction motor, as well as several forms of oscillators, the Tesla coil, and a wireless guidance system for ships. His genius and contributions to today's technology are only recently coming into the arena of public awareness and discussion. Looking at these examples, it reveals an unfortunate aspect of the cultural limitations on intelligent expression.

Intelligence is historically associated with, and identified by, how current social norms value and measure intelligence. We can conclude that how we measure and express intelligence is dependent on the perception of its value to society. Intelligence bias based on gender is one problem this book seeks to clarify and offer solutions to effectively manage across the LifeSpace. In this context, I characterize intelligence bias as the assumption that someone has limited capacity to develop intelligence because of their gender.

What is Your Choice?

To be only smart—which is really the difference between IQ and EQ, or book smarts versus common sense—limits your awareness and narrows your focus. To be intelligent is to see broadly and creatively while understanding that learning is a continuum and requires a high level of awareness. Intelligence is when we apply the correct balance of knowledge to the appropriate situation and the parameters of the environment, at the right moment in time. (#DIVAiqeq)

Maximize your capacity to use all forms of intelligence. Whether you are street smart, book smart, or use common sense and have a high EQ, boldly use them all to navigate through the range of simple to complex life decisions. Constantly self-develop using learning tools and personal assessments to inform more intelligent behavior and thinking that will get you to the level of awareness you seek.

Five Tips for Developing Intelligent Thinking and Behavior

1. Understand the difference between IQ, EQ, and EI.
2. Complete at least three personality assessments to identify your strengths and weaknesses compared to others. You can use the charts below to aid you. Personality assessments are not exact, they only provide information and guidance. Only you can determine the validity of the assessment to the extent that you agree or disagree with the results.
3. Create a self-development plan with action steps to strengthen the areas you would like to develop. The Leadership Self-Inventory form, included at the end of Chapter 18, is what I use to track my assessments and design actions for further self-development.
4. Discuss your self-development plan with a friend, coworker or supervisor for accountability.
5. Learn to practice desired behaviors and recommendations to put your assessment into action.

UNDERSTANDING THE RELATIONSHIP BETWEEN SUCCESS, IQ AND INTELLIGENCE

The table below lists corresponding ranges of IQ scores with intelligence. Research shows that half of IQ scores (50%) fall between 90 and 110. Genius or near-genius IQ is considered to start around 140 to 145 and less than a quarter of 1 percent of the population falls within this range.

Management and leadership research suggests that any one of us can be successful in life if we possess an above average range of intelligence. However, personality and motivation are also influencing factors that affect a person's ability to be successful or not. The source link to the below chart will allow you to test your range of intelligence. There is a fee and a no fee option to take the IQ test.

IQ Scale	
IQ (% of Population with this IQ)	**Interpretation**
Over 130 (2.1)	Very gifted
121 – 130 (6.4)	Gifted
111 – 120 (15.7)	Above average intelligence
90 – 110 (51.6)	Average intelligence
80 - 89 (15.7)	Below average intelligence
70 - 79 (6.4)	Cognitively impaired
Source: https://www.123test.com/interpretation-of-an-iq-score/	

THE FOUR-QUADRANT MODEL OF SOCIAL & EMOTIONAL INTELLIGENCE

The Four-Quadrant Model of Social & Emotional Intelligence: Social and emotional intelligence is the ability to be aware of our own emotions and those of others, *in the moment,* and to use that information to manage ourselves and manage our relationships.

	self	other
awareness	**Self-Awareness** • Emotional Self Awareness • Accurate Self Assessment • Personal Power	**Other Awareness** • Empathy • Situational/Organizational Awareness • Service Ethic
management	**Self Management** • Behavioral Self Control • Integrity • Innovation & Creativity • Initiative & Bias for Action • Achievement Drive • Realistic Optimism	**Relationship Management** • Communication • Interpersonal Effectiveness • Powerful Influencing Skills • Conflict Management • Inspirational Leadership • Catalyzing Change • Building Bonds • Teamwork & Collaboration

	- Resilience - Stress - Management - Personal Agility - Intentionality	- Coaching & Mentoring Others - Building Trust

Source:http://the-isei.com/Libraries/Site_Documents/SEI_Four_Quadrant_Model_6-10_-_Adult_Version.sflb.ashx

3
NEVER, NEVER, RELINQUISH YOUR POWER

"The most common way people give up their power is by thinking they don't have any." — *Alice Walker*

This is Kim and Ella's story. Kim is a thirty-year-old writer and web designer from Philadelphia and Ella is a bookstore/café owner in her late sixties. Kim is struggling to let go of limiting beliefs so she can confidently move forward in making decision that will have a positive impact on her life. A conversation with Ella about a local news article motivates her to find a life coach. Kim wears red eyeglasses that frame her heart-shaped face and she keeps her hair pulled back in a bun. She looks like an English teacher from the sixties. Their story is important because it illustrates the importance of letting go of limiting beliefs that hold back your power and can limit your future successes.

KIM & ELLA

It was a gorgeous morning in Philadelphia that was cool enough for me to sit and watch the new spring blossoms from the outdoor patio of my favorite café and country bookstore. At age thirty, everything was coming to me in small, bite-sized accomplishments. My first home in Center City was a reality. After five years on the job, I was now considered vested. I was also single again after three years of marriage and my decisions were all my own.

I came to the cafe fairly often and Ella and I had become quite familiar with each other. She usually stopped whatever she was doing to say hello, or personally bring over a refill of my favorite peppermint tea. As a single woman it was nice to be noticed. At least one person would be able to vouch for my existence if I died in a car wreck in the Amazon. Ella would be able to say, "she was such a pleasant young woman who loved to read classic novels, short story compilations, and fashion magazines." It was comforting to know that Ella would tell the media and notify concerned family and friends who had seen so little of me during my laser-focused pursuit of career ambitions.

Every Sunday I would sit outside on the veranda and order an herbal tea with a salad or sandwich. Ella and her husband owned the café. This was one of the reasons I supported them as an advocate for women-owned businesses. It was a sign of much needed freedom and self-empowerment. It gave me hope and fueled my energy to one day own a business.

Ella was an inspiration to me. She was a smart businesswoman, but I also liked her as a person. She enjoyed helping people and it seemed that she simply couldn't help herself. It gave her satisfaction, so much so that she didn't care if they were taking advantage of her generosity or not. If they needed it that badly, then fine, take it. The result was a reputation for providing extraordinary customer service. She would hold books for weeks, unpaid, and on occasion would call to ask if I would like her to have a newly released preorder dropped off on my doorstep when the weather was simply too cold to wander out.

Ella brought over a cup of hot peppermint tea and glanced at the headline of the paper lying on the table. She shook her head and said, "What a horrible misuse of trust."

Her always observing eye was correct. My peppermint tea had gotten cold and I was happy she'd brought over a fresh cup. But Ella's attention was quickly diverted by the day's headlines.

"You certainly have to be careful who you give up your power to." Ella said nodding at the newspaper. Then she glanced out into the store to check on her other customers. When no glances of need or frustrated expressions of an unfound book were sent her way, she continued.

"These are my friends who come into the store and insist on paying for a cup of tea," she whispered. Then they have the audacity to leave me a tip," Ella laughed. "I still don't understand why they do that. My overhead is paid for in that $2.50 cup of tea. I do feel terrible about it— the tips that is."

From our previous talks, I learned that Ella married later in life and delayed starting a family until one day, she realized it wouldn't happen. Time had passed. Decades later, in her third life, the bookstore gave her an opportunity to be productive and be her own boss. I believed it was in some ways a statement against the power and authority figures of her past.

Her comment about being careful who you give your power to, was in response to an article about a young woman who had been the victim of broken trust and abuse of power. It clearly affected Ella deeply.

Ella could easily be the librarian or the English teacher who graded you harshly and always asked you to do better. Her smooth salt and pepper hair fell to her shoulders. A hint of past coloring attempts formed a slight ring around her temple. She wore a long floral dress and canvas sneakers with ankle socks. A sixties flower child came to mind but somehow I sensed she never reached the peak of liberation that many women experienced during that time. But, maybe she had.

From the way Ella hovered, I could tell she had another story to tell me and I was happy to wait patiently for that teachable moment.

"Are you leaving soon?" She asked as she picked up my empty cup.

"I can stay for another hour," I answered. Ella gave me a grateful smile.

"Wonderful. I'll be back by then with a slice of delicious lemon loaf for both of us."

Ella then swept back into the cafe to start the process of preparing to close at noon for her half day on Sunday. I assumed it was her only day of rest and a fitting time since most of the businesses on the busy main street closed during the weekend and it was now after the morning church goers, or bible thumpers as my brother called them, had filed through. After she'd left, I sat contentedly in the sun and sipped my tea waiting for her to return.

At noon Ella promptly flipped the sign in the window to CLOSED. She then began to gather her receipts as the last few customers lined up for purchases or finished their last sip or last bite of biscuits. Her husband was rarely there on the weekends. From my conversations with Ella I knew that he handled the finances and inventory while she managed the kitchen, bookstore and customer service. They had two other employees who seemed to be volunteers or retirees looking to keep themselves busy. Their endless chatter and stories gave the place a nostalgic feel of story time at home around a warm crackling fire. Ella reminded me of Mrs. Lee, my favorite English teacher who always had a warm smile or an encouraging word for her students.

Ella circled back to me. I was her last task for the day, her last customer. She leaned over to peer into my cup of tea. The peppermint was still covering the bottom and still warm. She topped it off and replaced my plate of crumbs from a chocolate scone with a plate with a slice of lemon loaf. When she returned from the kitchen she took the seat across from me. She then began to tell her story.

"True wisdom comes to each of us when we realize how little we understand about life, ourselves, and the world around us. I know that I am intelligent because I know that I know nothing." – Socrates

The article Ella had such an immediate reaction to told the story of Leanne. She was a member of the church for nearly twenty years; she was and I assume, still is, Ella's friend.

Leanne was a member of Ella's church and a faithful patron for over ten years since the day Ella first brought her in. She had college-aged children but was going through a divorce from her husband. Her husband was the authority at home, her church was the authority in their lives, and her children were the authority on her future as a mother. She had gladly relinquished her power in all these roles.

When her marriage, ended, Leanne and her children went away to school, she turned to her pastor for guidance and purpose. However, what started as a woman seeking to rediscover herself following a midlife crisis turned into the biggest scandal the town had ever experienced. Over the next few years Leanne became a victim of sexual exploitation and abuse by not one member of the clergy, but several who demoralized her and convinced her that she could be of service through sexual encounters with these men. It gave new meaning to the phrase divine intervention. The abuse of power was now being exposed. Leanne had been sworn to tell no one, but following an incident where she needed medical attention, a psychiatrist was called in and during an intense session, Leanne opened up. The psychiatrist later, with her consent, reported the abuse. It was the talk of the town.

Ella felt guilty because she had known Leanne long before the incident.

When Ella finished her story, I looked at her in amazement then asked, "How do you think that can happen?"

Ella hesitated and then shifted as if to put herself into another place in time. "How old are you dear," she asked?

"I'm thirty." I answered in a tone laced with the worries passed on by my mother that convinced me I was at the end of my childbearing years.

"So young," Ella smiled. "Why do you come here alone?"

"I like the quiet, it helps me to think."

I wasn't so sure that I wanted to answer too many questions about my life. I took a sip of tea to allow a moment of diversion. Ella ran her fingers over her hair to smooth out a spot that went against the normal fall of her curly tresses.

"You're searching for something. The answer is somewhere in these books, but you'd probably be over 100 years old before you find the answers in all of them. Then you realize that time has changed and the context and characters are no longer quite the same."

Ella sighed deeply before continuing. "I grew up in the sixties in Arkansas where trust, authority, and power were all one in the same. For as long as I could remember, women were expected to abide by whatever form of authority or power was presented to us. Trust was defined very early as something you gave freely to everyone unless they were strangers. Unfortunately, there were no strangers in their small community in the south, just random faces that would pass through every now and again looking for work."

I imagined it was a time when woman still had to ask for her husband's permission to learn to drive or participate in a social club. For me, when it came to waiting for my "knight in shining armor, Prince Charming, and all-around good guy," I felt strongly that he would find me or we would at least find each other. For that reason, I decided to pursue my life and my interests to the fullest extent. I hadn't wanted to wait to really start living.

Ella's father was both power and authority in the home. He had power because he held the purse strings and emotional baggage that came with it. He had authority that he selected and delegated to her mother. He gave and removed authority as much as he wanted. One thing remained constant. No one ever questioned him.

"That gave him tremendous power to manipulate us in whatever way he chose," Ella said.

She believed that the accumulation of property, a career, and relationships was all part of living and growing the social connection that would become her identity.

Ella checked her watch. It was 1:00. She excused herself and went into the cafe. When she returned she had a glass of wine and a bright red book. Its pages were dog-eared and tattered. She placed it on the table.

"The nearest library in my town was thirty minutes away and nobody in those parts sold books like these. They were blasphemous. It questioned everything. It questioned me."

Ella took a sip of her wine then sat it on the table before she spoke. It was 1967 and she was only fourteen years old but very mature for her age.

"I knew I had less than two years to figure out another path or to prepare to get married and live a most certain future."

For Ella, the only way to change her path was to school or work. Women were starting to work more but not her mother. She said that was a different era for her. It was Ella's time to take advantage of the new movement for women and the right to work.

Ella decided she would study hard and find a way out. There was a swell of hope in the air. She heard it in the local discussions and read it in the newspapers. The pastor's sermons changed and became more assertive and threatening about a woman's role as wife, mother, and caretaker. It was blasphemous to ask for anything more than that. Ella picked up the book and weighed it in her hands.

"My sister gave me this book in 1969 as a sixteenth birthday present," Ella said. "She'd heard about it from one of her female in-laws. A librarian and confidante secretly ordered it and had it mailed marked confidential. My sister then read it, and went to great lengths to conceal it from our parents."

Ella showed me the cover. It was *The Feminine Mystique* by Betty Friedan. It was the original hard copy first published in 1963.

"After I read the book, I made a promise to myself to take control of my life. I wanted to travel, have new experiences and learn about myself. I decided to put off marriage as long as possible and I became a librarian. I saved for many years to take a vacation. When I turned twenty-four I decided it was time to take a trip to England." Ella's eyes grew wistful as she traveled back through the years. "The time to do it was now while I was still unmarried and without children. I was in a steady relationship, but we had never discussed anything beyond that."

Ella had planned it as a girls' trip. My boyfriend wasn't happy that I had made plans to travel without him and had not told him. She feared he would tell her parents, assume he had a say in it, or even worse, assume she needed his permission. She was correct on all three.

Her friends had always told her she was a realist. So, as a realist, it never occurred to her that as an unmarried woman, she would need to somehow qualify her life to accommodate a boyfriend's fears, insecurities or sense of ownership.

"He was free to make a real commitment at any time." Ella sighed then took a moment before continuing.

Ella struggled with the fears and concerns of her family who feared the unknown, which was just about everything outside of Arkansas. But she felt strongly that decisions for her life would be her own to make and she worked hard to broaden her choices.

Before long, she made plans to travel to London for vacation and five of her friends, all in their twenties, were thrilled to join her. They had never traveled overseas and this test of freedom was long overdue! They planned a year out and set deadlines for when deposits were due. Yet, one by one, everyone began dropping out for some reason—boyfriend, kids, jobs, or financial problems—all were excuses. This happened before when they planned to take a trip to Canada.

"I made a decision at that moment that if I waited for other people to complete my life, it would never happen and I would die without ever accomplishing my dreams," Ella said with a hint of sadness in her voice.

But, she knew it was simply not possible to live life to its fullest when you allowed other people to dictate the terms. Inevitably, you will see the future unfulfilled. Then, she made her choice.

"I decided I would go alone," Ella said. She then told her friend Leanne. She had been the last to bail out."

"Is that safe? Your boyfriend is not going to let you travel alone, is he?" Leanne asked as she gave me a disapproving look.

"I reminded her that I was a single woman who could afford to travel anywhere she pleased and that I didn't need anyone's permission."

That was one of the last times she saw Leanne before she found her living in Philadelphia. They had met over lunch weeks prior. It had been nearly 40 years.

"I was so happy to see her," Leanne said with a sincere expression of glee. "She was broken, she had regrets, but she was finally free to be who she wanted to be."

Ella then looked distant then smiled as her thoughts shifted to more recent memories from her circle of new and adventurous friends. People she would have never met and are now her eyes through which she sees a bigger and more colorful world.

London had truly been a liberating moment. Since then she continued to meet other women who travel alone. She had found that it wasn't so scary or rare. She was part of an inner circle of world travelers from all walks of life. And they were women of all ages. Her circle of friends grew to include single women who were even more adventurous than she had ever been. One of those women, Cynthia had embarked on a summer tour of Asia, Africa, and Europe. She decided to quit her job in banking after twenty years for the opportunity to completely free herself of 'all my baggage.' Ella looked proud and confident. I sensed there were secrets she wanted to tell. Maybe one day I would hear them.

Ella seemed to have unburdened herself after telling me her story. She picked up the book and looked at it for a long time.

"It's such a hard thing to question authority. This book gave me the courage to do it and eventually to leave everything I knew. It wasn't always easy, but I'm so glad I did."

Now, decades later, Ella is twice divorced and lives with her common-law husband.

"Before I traveled and learned about myself through my experiences, I was insecure and immensely trusting and giving. I've tried to tell everyone I meet to believe in and to trust in themselves, especially young women. And just as important, not to relinquish their power or authority."

Ella regretted that Leanne was taught to trust, implicitly and without question, the people who harmed her and betrayed her. They were taught the same thing and you want to believe in yourself ability to make your own decisions, but you begin to doubt yourself. Ella was hearing those little voices from her childhood, telling her that people in power and authority figures are the people who know what it best for you. Now life was coming come back to remind her that maybe it could have been different for her too. She was motivated once again to live and exercise her power of choice.

It was now well past 3:00 PM and the single glass of wine was long sipped and savored. It was just a matter of minutes before my stomach would start to grumble, signaling it was time for dinner. Ella's epiphany moment came at sixteen with a book that challenged her to change her future. She was lucky. Mine happened at thirty.

Women must learn to take ownership of their lives. No matter what the course, decide which path, how far you will go, and when to change course. From that moment forward, I decided I needed to prove something to myself. I would not make decisions based on fear. I decided that after I ruled out all of the reasons why I might not fully experience life by stepping out of my comfort zone, if fear was the last one standing, it was not good enough. I would go forward with life.

What is Your Choice?

To be smart is to effectively exercise power when it is assigned through the responsibilities of a role or a position of authority. To be intelligent is to understand that true power comes from within—it's your personal power. It is the manifestation of the ability to both influence and motivate others toward a mutually agreed upon outcome. Personal power is not punitive or threatening. (#DIVApower)

Live your life with little regret. The willingness to relinquish your power is a sign of insecurity and lack of confidence. Build confidence and the awesome wisdom that comes from experiencing life without self-sabotage and fear. Continue to challenge yourself to learn and do more. Increasing your range of experiences across your 4D LifeSpace will inform more intelligent decisions.

Seven Tips for Asserting Your Power

1. Recognize your core motivation and the personality traits and behaviors that attract people to you or push them away from you.
2. Seek to understand the conscious or latent motivation in others and its effect on your dreams and desires.
3. When you don't know, ask yourself, "What is my (and their) motivation?"
4. Engage in self-development activities that improve your ability to self-manage your emotional and social intelligence.
5. Move away from the details, the fine points, and the particulars (this is smart). Look to the objective. This is where the goals, outcomes and solutions can be found and where your power to motivate and influence others is best demonstrated (this is intelligent).
6. Ask for more authority.
7. Exercise personal power.

WHAT IS YOUR CORE MOTIVATION?

Each of us is motivated in different ways and those motivations are a product of our personality. As with other personality assessments and charts, the Core Motivation chart gives you an opportunity to explore what habits and emotions most reflect you. It is not unusual to have characteristics of more than one type. Read the chart and choose two that most describe you. The purpose of the chart is to aid in your personal growth by raising your level of self-awareness. When we better understand ourselves, we also gain a better understanding of our relationships with others and can create opportunities for personal improvement when challenges arise. The ability to manage ourselves and our relationships with others is an important aspect of emotional intelligence.

CORE MOTIVATION TYPES	
Type One: **THE PERFECTIONIST**	**Type Two:** **THE HELPER**
I strive for things to be perfect and in place. If I'm passionate about something, I work really hard and spend a lot of time on it. I want other things around me to be perfect, but I am mostly hard on myself. I am very critical of the things I do and I am very disappointed in myself when I make a mistake. I often have a lot of priorities on my plate, but I just want to improve my life and the lives of others. Oftentimes people follow my lead and I am comfortable in that leadership capacity. Whatever I have to do, it has to be done right and I will do what it takes to get there. Others might say I am intense or too serious at times, but I just like to be focused and I would rather relax when the work is done.	What really drives me is my ability to help others. I love doing things for somebody, especially if I know they will appreciate it. I feel like I know how best to help people because it's usually easy for me to determine their wants and needs. It might seem like I try too hard or am controlling at times, but it's just because I want to help in the best way. I get satisfaction out of putting others before myself, though sometimes that takes its toll when I don't focus on my own needs. I like when others recognize that I am there for them and I usually have a difficult time saying 'no.' I also place a huge emphasis on relationships. I give a lot of myself in hopes that others will recognize what I have given, and in turn will respect me for that. At the end of the day I hope that the people I help will

	be there for me when necessary.
Type Three: **THE DOER** I want to be the best I can be at what I do. Goals are important to me and I work hard at achieving them. I feel very successful when I meet my goals, and I want others to respect me for it. My mind works rather quickly and sometimes I can get irritable if something or someone seems to be working too slowly. Though I am personally competitive, I can also do well on a team and am well liked. I want to make a good impression on people and I care about how others view me. When I have a really passionate goal, I know just what to do to achieve it and stay motivated. I prefer to do only the things I am good at.	**Type Four:** **THE ARTIST** I like to express my emotions and I want others to understand me for who I am. I consider myself genuine and unique. I'm constantly seeking more in terms of my life and I try to evaluate and consider what is missing. I don't like to be misunderstood and sometimes people might mistake me for being dramatic or caring too much, but really I just want to express exactly how I feel. I like to get to know others on a deeper level and form real connections. I'm passionate about feelings and I want to accurately reveal myself to others.

Type Five: **THE THINKER**	Type Six: **THE FRIEND**
I love being the expert. Before I delve into something, I want to know as much as I can. I don't like to be wrong or corrected, which is why if I don't know something, I would rather not say it. I am happy to argue my points for what I believe is right, but if the facts don't support my idea, I will reconsider my idea. I often thrive on alone time and I like to think about my past experiences. I am pretty independent and I don't want to have to rely or depend on someone else. I crave information and knowledge and I am not shy in a group setting, where I can speak up and say what I know and express what I want. Overall, I am a simple person and my life is rather straightforward.	I like to be prepared for the worst. Often I envision worst-case scenarios so that I know just what to do in case they actually happen. I have a creative imagination and a somewhat odd sense of humor. I can be unsure of people in authority, especially if I don't trust them. Once I trust someone and have explored an idea, I will be very loyal. When it comes to new ideas, the first thing that usually comes to mind is what could go wrong. I would rather think it through before accepting it for face value. I am not much of a follower, especially when it comes to ideas, because I can easily pick out why I disagree with it.

Type Seven: **THE OPTIMIST**	Type Eight: **THE DEFENDER**
I enjoy life at a fast pace. I like to create many options for myself and future plans and keep many options open. I shy away from negative emotion and I hate feeling bored or trapped with my life. If I am upset over something, I don't want to dwell on it. Sometimes I will get really excited over something rather quickly but then eventually I will get bored with it and forget about it or drop it. Often times I will start things that don't quite get finished. At the same time, I am very optimistic and I believe life is a ride that is meant to be enjoyed. When I have several options that I can choose from, I have a hard time deciding because I want them all.	I like to be in control as much as possible. I am very blunt and honest because I want the things to be clear. It frustrates me when I feel like someone is conniving or unfair. At times I might seem controlling but I just want to take charge and keep things going smoothly. I try to hide my weaknesses because I feel vulnerable when someone else knows what they are. That being said, I think we should still recognize our weaknesses and do something about them. I would rather get something done on my own than be told what to do, which is why I sometimes have a hard time following orders from authority. I won't always respect a person of authority upfront, but when I do, I am much more willing to follow directions from them.

Type Nine: **THE PEACEMAKER** I like things to be peaceful and happy. I tend to avoid conflict and confrontation. Sometimes I can't even recognize exactly what I want so I just go with the flow, especially in group settings. When I do know what I want, I might still agree with someone even if it goes against that. I might get angry at myself, but I don't like getting angry at other people, or when people are angry at each other. I have a kind heart and I know it can be taken advantage of. When I really need to I know how to stand up for myself. I am good at seeing multiple sides to a situation, both pros and cons.	

Another perspective on human motivation that influences our personality and motivates us to behave in certain ways is taken from looking at what we desire.

REISS' 16 BASIC DESIRES[ix]

New Theory of Motivation: A List of REISS' 16 BASIC DESIRES	
1. Acceptance, the need for approval	Acceptance
2. Curiosity, the need to learn	Curiosity
3. Eating, the need for food	Eating
4. Family, the need to raise children	Family
5. Honor, the need to be loyal to the traditional values of one's clan/ethnic group	Honor
	Idealism
	Independence
6. Idealism, the need for social justice	Order
7. Independence, the need for individuality	Physical activity
	Power
8. Order, the need for organized, stable, predictable environments	Romance
	Saving
9. Physical activity, the need for exercise	Social contact
10. Power, the need for influence of will	Social status
	Tranquility
11. Romance, the need for sex	Vengeance
12. Saving, the need to collect	
13. Social contact, the need for friends (peer relationships)	
14. Status, the need for social standing/importance	
15. Tranquility, the need to be safe	

16. Vengeance, the need to strike back/to win	
Source: http://psychology.wikia.com/wiki/16_basic_desires_theory_of_motivation	

4
QUESTION AUTHORITY

"Knowledge is having the right answer. Intelligence is asking the right question." — Unknown

Leslie is a twenty-two-year-old pre-med student from Denver who was seeking life coaching to improve her toxic relationship with her mother. Leslie is a smart and witty brunette with a strong personality. She's everyone's friend and the girl next door. Her story is important because it underscores the struggle to claim ownership and authority over our own lives, particularly within familial relationships.

LESLIE

"Do you really want what is best for me, mother, or what's best for you?" Leslie had finally said it out loud and her frustration came out in a stressed tone weigh down with the emotional exhaustion that came from years of distress stemming from her mother's relentless attempts to manage her life from cradle to grave.

Mrs. Baker sat across from her daughter and smoothed an invisible crease from her powder blue silk bath robe. She rarely bothered to get dressed or to do her hair and makeup when her daughter visited, unless she came with her college friends. This conversation had been going on for an hour now, as soon as Leslie walked in the front door and received the usual cool kiss and firm hug. Things were changing. Leslie was becoming more and more defiant. Despite the veiled attempts at sincerity, her mother's dismissive tone also revealed that she too was changing. She had lost interest in appearances and no longer subscribed to the rules of social graces and manners, that "Dear Abby," tea party etiquette, and social-club parenting required.

The debates had started early, somewhere in Leslie's junior year of high school when colleges started sending information after she scored in the top national percentile of the standardized assessment test. However, Leslie's excitement was quickly dampened by her mother, Sharon.

"Leslie, I don't think college is for you. I mean what would you do? It's not like you were the smartest in your class. Only the salutatorian and valedictorians go to the top universities. And it's so expensive. You don't even have a car."

These were reasonable arguments.

"Why don't you think about marriage first? You'll make a great mother, I know you will." Sharon finished with a small smile.

It seemed the whole world was lined up to support my mother's point of view; the preservation of the so-called traditional family. Women with a college education were not so traditional. It was constantly reinforced in church-selected Bible verses that told us men were the head of the household or that children must honor thy mother and father, or to reject worldly things. Well what if your mother and father are abusing you, what then? And what was worse was the underlying message that this was how we needed to distinguish ourselves from those other people. The ones with broken homes, gays, the minorities, those other religions, those other people, it went on and on.

I had many friends in school but to bring any of them home turned into an interrogation from my mother when they left. "Who is she, where does she live, who are her parents, what do they do?" If the neighborhood where they lived or their parents' occupation was unacceptable, I was warned to be careful. It didn't matter if he or she was smart or talented. Their zip code gave enough information for my parents to shut them out. If I refused, that week's sermon would surely be about honoring thy mother and father, with a touch of fire and brimstone to bring out the right amount of fear. It was convincing and even frightening, to a child. It was not so convincing to a maturing young woman.

For years, I struggled with the sad and sometimes angry mix of emotions that I inevitably felt when I spoke with my mother.

While there was this sense of pride and desire for nothing but the best for her daughter, Leslie knew her mother's measure of what was best for her child's life had everything to do with what was best for her -- Mrs. Sharon Baker. It was never said aloud or discussed. For Leslie it was an accumulation of choices made, that in hindsight did not reap the benefits she, herself, had wanted. Instead it had turned out exactly as expected for her mother. Mrs. Baker always benefitted the most.

Eventually, Leslie graduated in the top five percent of her high school class and entered college with freshmen coursework already completed. She had invitations to visit Ivy League schools, but Mrs.

Finkelstein, the name Leslie called her mother behind her back, convinced her to attend the university closest to home.

> *"Character is higher than intellect. A great soul will be strong to live as well as think."—Ralph Waldo Emerson*

Sharon's current married name was Mrs. Baker, before it was Mrs. Stephens, before that it was Mrs. Schwartz, and before that it was her maiden name, Ms. Brown. Leslie assigned her the name Mrs. Finkelstein as a representation of her true character which, she would say to her amused friends, was a cross between Tinker Bell and Frankenstein.

On one hand, my mother is the daughter of my loving grandparents and the child who wanted to be a good fairy when she grew up, not the high-society person she had become through the spoils of broken homes, broken marriages, and the callous actions needed to come out on top. She was smart, sassy, and guarded. My father was to be her fourth and final "traditional" marriage. I was the last of three children.

"You should attend school here right in Colorado and live at home." My mother told me repeatedly. "You'll save money."

The thought of staying at home and being dictated to for another day, much less four years, made me cringe.

My heart was set on California. The state university's medical program was in the top ten percent of all medical schools. This worked well with the fact that I wanted to live near the beach and in a climate totally different from Denver, Colorado. I also knew I needed the distance away from my mother to find my independence. I was still unsure of my undergraduate specialty but my mom already had that figured out.

"I have no need of another doctor in the family. But, what I do need is a hairstylist." Yes, my mother actually said that to me. And she was serious. I was shocked.

There was not even the appearance of concern about my career dreams or aspirations. For what it's worth, I realized in that moment that people are people. They can only change who they are if they want too. Even as children, our nature is what it is. It's not our place to change it, but to acknowledge it in the face of our own lives. If we are selfish, conniving, dishonest people before becoming parents, then we will surely be the same afterwards unless we make the hard choice to change it. If we are caring, compassionate and thoughtful that is how we will be as parents.

Unfortunately, we're not all attuned enough at an early age to know if our parents are pathological liars, or if our birth was a continuation of a scheme, or if they genuinely love and care for us. I certainly didn't know the person my mother really was because she'd kept her so well hidden. One person who would know though, was her mother, my grandmother.

I once asked her why my mother had so few real friends.

"Oh, I've never known your mother to care about anything but money, dear," was grandma's casual reply. "Sometimes having genuine friends is a casualty of that."

My relationship with my grandmother had grown closer over the past few years. When I was younger I didn't know why grandma was guarded when she was around us or why her relationship with my mother was also strained. The answer came during her sixty-fifth birthday party, which was filled with friends and family. As we all gathered around her, she blew out the candles on her cake then she looked around the room and admitted, that for much of her life she had been a "certified alcoholic" and was glad to celebrate another birthday sober.

At that point, she'd been sober for more than fifteen years. There was no intervention or long period of recovery. She told us that one day, she just stopped drinking. Today at seventy, all of her demons have long been exorcised and she had little patience for nonsense. I imagined my mother had never fully forgiven her. She never spoke ill of my mother and I never asked about their relationship. But, today was different, I needed her advice. I was beginning to not like my mother and I needed to turn to someone for advice.

We are not all brave enough to distance ourselves from our parents. The best we can do is to be painfully honest about what our parents are capable of and to adjust or lives accordingly to receive the least amount of disruption to or dreams and happiness. To that end, I compromised and attended the in-state university but I chose to live on-campus.

Five years later, I graduated from the University of Colorado with a degree in Biology. I decided I wanted to be a medical scientist but would take a year off to work and teach inner city kids. I had three job offer letters before the date of my commencement.

"So where do you think you'll end up?" Mrs. Finkelstein asked me one day over the phone.

"I think I'll take the slot in Miami, Florida," I answered. My eyes were already rolling up to the ceiling in anticipation of the polite suggestion of another option.

"Where are the others located?"

"St. Louis and Oakland." I braced for the argument that would present her clear choice.

"Well what's in Florida?"

I was prepared. The beach argument was going to be weak with the California coastline just over a two-hour flight.

"They have no sales tax there," I replied. "And, when I look at all of the financial numbers, it is the best offer."

My mother went straight for the heart. "You have friends here and you're in a relationship. Have you discussed this with him?"

I was maturing and my friends were now my own and not the ones my parents chose to be in my life. They had been eclipsed by new people who brought with them the fulfilling gifts of experiences and understanding that I needed at this point in my life. They touched my heart and soul and added value to my life experience. They had entered my life of their own free will and I had to stand up for my decision to keep them in my life. Mom wouldn't understand that.

When family is Not enough, Find Relationships That Empower You and Give What You Need to Succeed

College was a great experience because I began to see things more broadly and from many different perspectives that I didn't even know existed. My new friends had a lot to do with that.

Jennifer would be one of those friends for life. We met during our freshman year. I was very angry when I first met Jennifer. I was angry at life and the stress of dealing with my parents' demands.

I was also a bit jealous. She was from Florida and her mom came with her the first week of classes to make sure she had everything she needed. Wasn't this the same thing I wanted from my mother? Why wasn't her mom afraid of letting go of her daughter? Why was she not trying to control her, or be delusional in her expectations?

What I later learned was that Jennifer's mom was all of those things. However, she compromised by taking Jennifer to school and then visiting with her for those first weeks to allay her fears of letting go. After that she called every night for months. It must have been difficult, but she respected her daughter's decisions as Jennifer made her own college and career choices.

Through the eyes of other daughters, I became more aware of my mother as a person. I met moms she didn't know, those who were not her friends, who did not live in our neighborhood. I met mothers who didn't know me as an extension of my family. They were different, very different from my mother. And to them I was an individual, and they judged me on my own merit.

I visited Jennifer's home in Maryland many times over numerous spring breaks. I became a part of her extended family and she became a lifelong friend. One day I asked her mom if she was at peace with her daughter being so far away.

"It's her life, her career, her choice," she answered. Her mother offered no additional explanation, there was no need. The thought of her kids growing up was something she had made peace with long ago.

That was when I had an epiphany. That's it! I thought, this is my choice.

Now, the moment of reckoning was here. The discussion about my first real job had shifted into a discussion yet again about what was best for my mother and my boyfriend. The conversation continued.

"Mother, I'm single and I have no intention of getting permission from anyone about the plans I have for my life until I'm engaged with a wedding date set. And that includes you."

For a moment there was silence on the other end of the phone. I was ready for the reply.

"Okay little girl." Mrs. Finkelstein said, reluctantly relinquishing control.

I smirked as she changed the subject. There was no doubt this discussion would continue another time—and soon.

I believe that was the first time Mrs. Finkelstein realized I was a young woman, not a controllable extension of her life as she saw it. I was now functioning independently of her orchestration and I felt free to let her know it. From that moment on, I was no longer two years old, I was twenty-two.

Over the years, I'd hear other stories of young women fighting for their own voice against parents seeking to direct them toward their idea of happiness. I read of a female military colonel who became a soldier despite her mother's casual dismissal of her dreams. When her daughter told her what she wanted to do, she replied, "You'll have to relocate. Who is going to take care of me?"

I kept that article to remind me that I wasn't alone.

Then there was a woman who called a popular radio show therapist to seek help in convincing her daughter to go through with her wedding. This was despite that fact that her daughter had confided that her fiancé was abusive to her. The concerns of the bride-to-be's mother led her to call the radio show on behalf of her daughter.

What the therapist eventually wrestled out of her were the many mental distortions and limiting beliefs she held that would lead her to the delusional conclusion that her daughter could overlook the abuse if she would only consider the benefits her marriage would bring to the family.

I imagined he was the man of her *mother's* dreams. Her daughter would have to sacrifice her happiness and health for her mother's dream of the perfect son-in-law.

It gave new meaning to phrase, "take one for the team."

Intelligent women know their parents' demons very well and rarely confront them, nor should they. They simply smile, appreciate these sources of life's experiences that inform their perspective and decisions in a way that really adds value to their dreams and goals.

These "aha" moments are so rewarding. They are better than "I told you so" moments, because they confirm our inner intuition and unexplainable emotions that weigh heavily on our minds. These feelings stem from knowledge of what is real and what we know, and affirms our inherent beliefs, in contrast to what we have been taught or told. They affirm our inherent beliefs.

What is Your Choice?

To be smart is to know the source of the information, the formula to the equation, and the answer to the question. To be intelligent is to understand that knowledge is gleaned through broader thinking in context that provides deeper meaning and insight. It requires nonlinear thinking that respects authority while challenging assumptions through inquiry and advocacy for truth. (#DIVAquestionauthority)

Power and authority are mutually exclusive but are instinctive bullying tactics for those with self-serving and personal interests. Know the limits of inherited or assigned authority and question your beliefs, values and ambitions, and to what end authority is necessary in meeting a valid purpose. There is no blind authority, even when dealing with our parents or family. To be intelligent is to know that power is given. It is your choice to relinquish it under any circumstance.

Seven Tips to Rightsizing your Relationships

1. Find your tribe. Gain confidence in yourself and your ideas by finding your community. One that nurtures and embraces curiosity, new ideas, information sharing and open dialogue in safe, healthy and open environment.
2. Own your character and personality. Practice empathy while becoming knowledgeable enough to eloquently defend your choices.

3. Name the personality you have difficulties with and share the name with its owner. It is the person, not the personality, you want to build the relationship with.
4. Exercise the art of asking curious questions.
5. Seek information and advice from creative and nontraditional sources for a refreshing perspective.
6. Put yourself out there! Invite experiences and relationships that test your capacity to think and learn.
7. Design your own wisdom circle. This is your personal executive board for counsel and advice. Rotate in new people as often as needed, and as your life progresses and you grow and mature.

MY WISDOM CIRCLE

There are nine individuals in my Wisdom Circle. It's okay to double up if there are people who give great advice in specific areas. For example, one of your moms can be a business owner, a former elected official, and your birth mom who isn't familiar with either of the other areas of knowledge, but who gives great practical advice. These moms represent older, wiser women and can also include your birth mother and even a best friend's mom or a woman who you see in that role regardless of whether she has children.

Having a second wisdom circle to help with specific goals is also acceptable. For example, in forming business relationships a trusted peer and colleague and business savvy mom can also be included in that wisdom circle. My wisdom circle is evolving to include women I don't know personally, but follow them online because of specific leadership or relatable traits I wish to adopt and emulate. My latest addition is Soledad O'Brien and her PowHERful Foundation.[x]

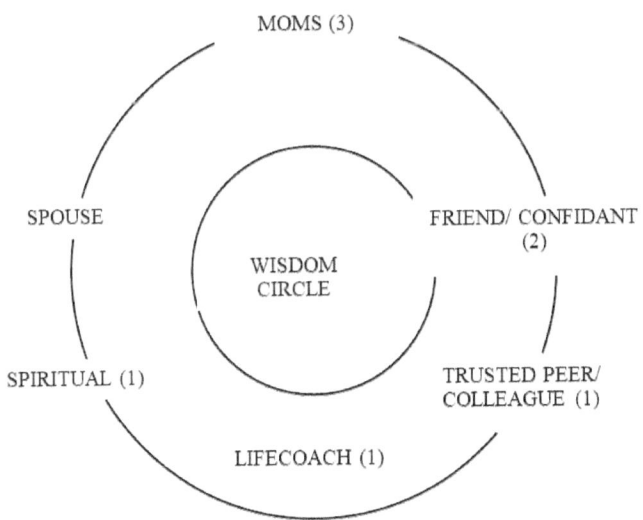

5
MAKE PEACE WITH YOUR SEXUALITY

"The highest form of human intelligence is to observe yourself without judgment." – Jiddu Krishnamurti[xi]

Amanda is a thirty-four-year-old deputy inspector general in San Diego. She is a multi-racial, all-American girl who tells her story through the experiences of her older sister, Angela. Amanda was seeking help to address negative self-perceptions and irrational thinking that prevented her from forming deep relationships. This story shows the cycle of negative thinking and the importance of releasing judgment, reframing, and letting go of limiting self-perceptions.

AMANDA

"Amanda, you stay away from those little boys." That was the only advice my father ever gave me and I must have been no more than eight years old at the time. It was a bit early, but I guess he needed to say it at some point and he chose sooner rather than later. The only other advice my father gave me was a stern warning not to kick the cat when I was ten. I suppose I was annoyed or just having a rotten day. My father and I were lounging on the porch watching the cars go by like so many other people did to pass the time on a hot day in the country. While I was nearing the point of rocking myself off to sleep, my dad's adopted stray decided to brush against my leg. It wasn't on impulse, but on purpose that I gave it a deliberate kick. My father was not pleased. It was the first and last time I remember him ever raising his voice to me. My dad was the most pleasant person ever; he never laid a hand on me. I was also his only child. His advice was important to me. I never kicked the cat or any cat again. I didn't fare so well with his advice about boys. My father passed away when I was fifteen. By the time I entered college, I really needed his advice.

My half-sister Angela was another story completely. Like me, she was average in high school, she wasn't a popular student and didn't care to be. She was average in everything with possibly the exception of her appearance. She was 5'4" and loved to wear tight jeans and spotless white sneakers, though her style was more tomboy than cheerleader. Her hair was very thick and coarse and had been cut short into a neat boyish style after years of over processing.

I remember her coloring, processing, extending, straightening, and braiding for what seemed like hours a day when we were younger. Mom either didn't notice or didn't care as long as she didn't have to do it. By the age of fourteen, Angela had finally given in to the realization that her breaking and split ends were best managed short. She rarely wore dresses and avoided lace and feminine clothing. In contrast, I loved bows and frilly dresses. My favorite outfit though were low-rise jeans with cut-off tops that left my belly button exposed. Any slimming top would do. I used to love wearing my grandmother's old prom dress to school. It was sleeveless with a tight bodice and short ballerina skirt. The peach color popped against my golden brown skin. I would put my long hair into two knots that looked like Mickey Mouse ears. I'd then slip on a pair of black three-inch heels. It was a brave statement of independence for a ninth grader. I loved it.

I loved all things Mariah Carey, who was huge at that time. I wrote my senior paper on one of her songs, "Butterfly". "Spread your wings and prepare to fly for you have become a butterfly," was my favorite verse. I studied Gloria Steinem, Nikki Giovanni, and Angela Davis, adored Kirstie Alley, but I *loved* Mariah. I was drawn to trailblazing women. My favorite book was Homer's *The Iliad* and *The Odyssey*. I indulged in fantasy and dreamed that I was a goddess.

My sister, Angela loved sports and was an excellent runner. Track season was the only thing I really looked forward too. Our family was very poor. At the beginning of each school year we received a week's worth of clothes, two pairs of shoes, and sets of T-shirts and blue jeans. We did laundry weekly to save water in the apartment. We sometimes had to wear clothes twice before we could wash them so it was important not to get them too dirty. Our separated, not-yet-divorced mother of four lived a government subsidized, church-filled life.

Angela was the oldest of four, and I was the third in between two boys, Gary and Lionel. At seventeen, she was about to experience the most defining moment in her teenage life.

"They boys at school are saying I'm a lesbian!" Angela said angrily, near tears.

She was my guardian, the person who always came to my defense when someone bullied or teased me. I was usually the one getting picked on, not her. The girls in class seemed to envy my status as the teacher's pet. I always brought home good grades and the teachers would ask me to participate in school plays, class projects, and clubs. My favorite volunteer assignment was delivering the morning announcements over the intercom. The home teacher's polite proclamation of a job well done was usually followed by smirks of annoyance by the other girls in class.

I never paid attention to the boys. My sister and I were both quiet and had few friends. Angela loved sports and the outdoors. I preferred to read and write songs.

"Who cares what people think? They don't even know you." I said in the nonchalant tone my mother despised.

Angela's anger grew more intense as she raised her voice. She always seemed so in control when she faced off against my bullies. At that time I didn't know that she was often in tears from our mother's verbal and physical abuse.

As the oldest, Angela usually took the full brunt of our mother's wrath. During her emotional outbursts Mom would lash out at Angela and hit her with anything within reach. Peach tree switches, pots and pans, and belts. My brothers and I had to watch helplessly or else we'd face the same fate. Sometimes it seemed to be almost daily. When my mother had a boyfriend, we were often left at home alone. It was a great time because we weren't in constant fear. But the moment we heard the sound of a car pulling into the driveway, we would run and hide. It would be our mother or the rare visit of an aunt or cousin. My sister took whatever mood mom brought home. The thick fabric of her tight-fitting jeans minimized the appearance of welts and hid the discolored bruises on her legs.

During her junior year, rumors began to spread that Angela didn't like boys. I heard the rumors and said nothing. It didn't seem important or relevant. I knew people were curious about us and this was the first full assault on our closed, private family. I guess we weren't normal and it was clear as evident from the rainbow of our complexions and how close we all were in age that pre-told our story. My brother and sister were eleven months apart and looked completely different.

Our mother was the product of a biracial father of Irish-African descent and a mother of African descent. While she appeared to be of biracial heritage, none of her children resembled her. My father was also biracial, Native and African American, a Seminole; even though the tribal councils didn't recognize those Native Americans of African descent.

Angela's father was my mother's husband and my dad; he was swarthy, tall and handsome. His skin was a deep chocolate. One day I heard him say I wasn't his child and then he stormed out.

Later, I discovered that my real father was twenty years my mother's senior. Sometimes I would see a strange man parked outside of our home. My mother would go out to speak to him; the man would leave after ten minutes or so. I met him for the first time when I was seven years old. I craved fudge when I saw him. That was the color of his eyes. For seven years he was off and on in my life. It's a curious thing that the only advice he ever gave me was to stay away from boys.

That is part of our story and the rumors about my sister's sexuality undoubtedly were based on the fact that we were strange, quiet, and stayed to ourselves. My sister and I didn't have much to say to boys.

As the rumors grew Angela became more insecure about her femininity. She decided that instead of trying to behave more like a girl, she would overtly demonstrate how much she liked boys. After all, she was a tomboy and I guess between the two, acting more like a girl was the least appealing choice.

The door to wisdom is knowing yourself – Unknown

"I love watching football. Just look at their butts in those tight uniforms." Angela would declare.

It was a Saturday and we were watching our favorite college team. Mom was rarely home on the weekends. As long as the house was spotless, we felt free to relax and enjoy our time together. The boys were out on yet another one of their adventures. That consisted of either squirrel hunting or bicycling the nearly two miles to play basketball on the only public basketball court.

I had not noticed any butts. I looked at the television to see for myself.

"I guess." I replied and went back to reading. She was watching the offensive line setup before the snap. So I suppose there was a line of butts. I liked the mascots on the team's helmets more than their butts.

The rumors at school and now on the school bus persisted, as did Angela's new attitude. It didn't seem to be working though, especially without a boyfriend to claim. I was convinced that the boys just wanted to have sex with her so they made her choose between accepting the rumors or receiving constant sexual harassment. It wasn't much of a choice.

At that time, I didn't understand the power of insecurity and the lack of self-esteem and self-confidence, particularly to a teenager in high school. Within a year the bullying and harassment worked and my sister changed.

Angela became pregnant, was off the track team, and had to finish the last semester of the senior year at home. She was embarrassed and ashamed. For the first time, my mom seemed to empathize with her. She too had become pregnant at seventeen and dropped out of high school. I remember Mom telling the story of how her great grandmother made the decision for her.

"Nana told me I had to marry him." She said in a sad, regretful voice.

By then, her mother, my grandmother, was not around much. As a teenager in high school, my mom and her two sisters were being raised by their sixty-year-old grandmother in a three-bedroom house with no working plumbing.

Like Mom, Angela was eight months pregnant when her class graduated. She didn't attend but the seventeen-year-old father did. The boys in her class had started the rumor and eventually what seemed like the entire student body became willing enablers while the teachers pretended not to be aware. As I think back, we never told our mother what was happening. She never had "that talk" with us. By the time we got our periods, we already knew what to do. Our mom didn't seem to notice. For us, it didn't matter.

Angela gave birth to a baby boy, the father showed up sporadically as the child became a young boy. My sister eventually married an insurance salesman but within five years and two kids of their own they were divorced. She found out that he had second wife in another state. Angela moved back in with our mother.

We have it set in our minds that inspiration only comes in positive forms. Inspiration can also be found in negative reinforcement. I chose to use my misfortunes as a motivating tool to get to a better place. All I needed to do was to see through the moment. It always bothered me that Angela allowed bullies, whose names she no longer even remembers, to manipulate her sexuality and start a path that would direct the entire course of her life. I suppose she was first my mom's victim and the choice to give into rumors was a comfortable space for her. Her sexuality after all is hers, and no one can dictate that to us. We are who we are.

That condensed view of my childhood experience was ten years ago and I had stumbled through it to become a liberated college graduate with a master's degree in public policy. A survivor of my upbringing I was now working in a profession that I loved as an inspector general for a large municipality. But one day, the lessons from my past came back to me when I received a call from Donna, a distraught woman who felt abandoned by her fiancé.

"I don't know what's going on," Donna screamed into the phone. "He's not emailing or calling me like he used to. Now I have no money for the wedding."

Donna had admitted earlier that she had gotten engaged to have sex. I quickly found out during the call that sex was just one item on the list of dysfunctions that characterized the relationship between her and her fiancé. I was her fiancé's supervisor and this was none of my business except that she had called the state attorney's office to file a complaint against our employee.

"He owes me money," she continued. "He agreed that he would help pay for the expenses."

I eventually got Donna off the phone but her admission stuck with me. I had the same struggles with sexuality. My mother made sure that we went to church three to four times a week. Part of that preaching included a fire and brimstone message on the virtues of virginity. It made this one aspect of our human makeup the most important asset of our lives. I had to hold on to my virginity for dear life. For me, it had not been difficult to remain a virgin, but instead it had been extremely difficult to keep focus on other things while practicing this virtue. This became increasingly more difficult in college.

I imagined that Donna had suffered that same difficulty and chose to get engaged as a trade-off for that relief. In contrast, I eventually reached a breaking point and chose to simply let it go so that I could get on with the rest of my life. Although I sometimes question my choice of with whom or how, I've never questioned that it was a good choice. For the first time, I began to see life in a broader more appreciative and nonjudgmental way. I felt liberated and empowered.

As I reflected on my sister, on Donna, and the decisions I had to make, I felt a reoccurring sadness that I couldn't come to terms with. The power of my sister's sexuality was something she was unaware of and because of that she was mistreated and used to the extent that she turned her power over to others. My personal determination not to be led by my sexuality empowered me to let go of its control over my planning and decision making. I gave up my virginity willingly and freely on my own terms and it was the most freeing moment of my life. After speaking with Donna it was clear that she was raised with the same belief that my mother endured nearly half a century ago, that her sexuality was a marital dowry. Her choice was to use her sexuality as a condition for money and security offered by a man she barely knew.

There was something similar happening in this modern, 21st century global environment of sexuality that I was trying very hard to understand. There seemed to be the same issues and problems with sexual harassment and gender, but among different and same sexes of all pairings and social groups.

I decided to confide in David, my boss and mentor. I didn't know how he would react but his words were helpful and made a big difference in my life.

"Life is life," David said. "It comes in many degrees and variations."

He explained to me that to the same extent there exists a range of people with vast degrees of intelligence from outright ignorant, to stupid, to smart, wise, and everything in between. The varying range of sexuality is just as complex. His advice from a business and human perspective was, "Your job is to understand and appreciate all of it." David, then added in the self-deprecating way he used to reduce the intimidation others often felt in his presence. "I'm not smart enough to think I can figure it all out. Nor do I care to be that kind of ass." He finished with a smile.

I remember thinking, "I think he just called me an ass."

David is still one of the people I most adore to this day. At that time he was seventy-three years-old, and divorced more times than he cared to mention. Because of him, I gained much needed perspective and wisdom on the similarities in basic human intelligence and gender realities in nearly half the time.

I can't fully put into words just how special he was and still is to me.

What is Your Choice?

To be smart is to know that a healthy heart and mind is one that is guilt free and open to forgiveness. Intelligence is to understand that the power of self-forgiveness and self-transformation aligns with your authentic self and is a measure of the work required to write, revise and rewrite your personal legend. (#DIVAmakepeace)

Choose to move forward. You were born with personality and sexuality, but neither define you or control your life. Managing self and sexual awareness is part of your maturing intelligence that requires self-forgiveness, peace and balance. Keep these two vulnerabilities in perspective with all of the equally important areas of your 4D LifeSpace. The value of one does not outweigh the other, nor do they define you or dictate your future.

Six Tips for Writing Your Personal Legend

1. Put the problem and the past behind you. Pick a future target such as a specific goal or outcome and focus on actions and solutions that will lead you there.
2. Open your mind to opportunities, they are all around you.
3. Forgive yourself and others. Write down the lessons learned.
4. Write down your goals and adopt a personal mantra that anchors you in a positive mindset.
5. Envision your desired future self and give her a name. Write down her personality, strengths, values, and vision then map out the road that got her there.
6. Close the door to energy that drains you and slows you down. Clear out the clutter and the noise around you that contributes to negative self-talk, low energy, and unhealthy environments.

6
FIND YOUR AUTHENTIC SELF

"The more you know yourself, the more clarity there is. Self-knowledge has no end—you don't come to an achievement, you don't come to a conclusion. It is an endless river." — *Jiddu Krishnamurti*

Rita (short for Margarita) is a thirty-two-year-old bank teller and pre-law student from Chicago. She is an ambitious first generation Mexican American who was seeking coaching to help create a vision and a clarity of purpose for her life. Lacey is a twenty-six-year-old management analyst and marathon runner from Nashville who was in need of clarity to address self-doubt and insecurity in her relationship with her boyfriend, Brett. These stories are important because they capture the conflict many people experience when seeking powerful change or to reclaim control over their life.

The discovery of your authentic self, the exercise and fluid expression of thinking and behaviors that reflect who you really are and your personal desires, is known in professional and life coaching as the breakthrough moment. That is when we begin to speak and hear our own voice. It's that moment of confidence, of self-actualization, and self-awareness that leads to discovery of a higher order of being and doing. In order of Maslow's Hierarchy of Needs, self-actualization is the realization of self-awareness, freedom, honesty, and trust.

I know many people who remember their worst critic and live by their last words. "You can't write." "You can't play music." "You can't dance." "You're stupid." "You'll never amount to anything." And so it goes throughout our lives as we await validation we rarely get! But, equally as harmful are well-meaning parents and friends who contribute false positive statements as a form of encouragement to motivate us to get to a future state of being. "You're smart." "You're talented." "You're beautiful." "You're special." These may sound like wonderful motivating words. The problem is the context in which these accolades are given. Special moments of praise need to be encouraged with evidence and shared meaning, not wishful thinking.

The longer you go through life, the more people will have an opinion to share about you. Some offer them freely but with either the intentions to help, to influence, or to hurt. The most painful ones, the ones that really stuck came from those we cared about, and wanted to care about us in return.

It wasn't until I was in my late twenties that I realized they had one thing in common. They were seeing me based on their own reality, perceptions, expectations, and experience or lack of experiences, and not by mine. There's an arrogance that precedes them.

RITA

My first lesson about the power of other's influence on our life choices came when I was applying to law school. I was single and very independent and thought I knew everything I needed to have a successful academic career. An important part of that confidence came through my affiliation with the right student leadership programs and professors who mentored me. The other was having the right student alliances to support a future in the field of law or government. I was a member of the student government council, the student leadership fraternity, and a member of a sorority. Each provided academic support through free tutors, sharing old tests and cliff notes, mentorship, and peer group support. They also offered new relationships and gave referrals through my peer's family members who already had established careers.

Although I was not yet confident in who I was as a person, I focused on being confident in my career pursuits. I'd later find that one could not succeed without the other. I had to be confident in my own skin as well as in the suit I would wear to the office.

That lesson came during an open house held in south Florida for prospective law school students. I remember that it was around the time when issues of reverse discrimination, affirmative action, and college quotas were in the news. I even think a U.S. senator had referred to the location as a third-world country. Coming from Chicago, I was excited to have been invited because I was very interested in incorporating more cultural diversity into my academic learning. The U.S. is a melting pot and as a Mexican American, I embraced it. I wanted to be a bilingual attorney.

The forum was mainly for women and other minorities. It was organized by local law associations and panelists representing a diverse range of lawyers, judges, academics, and law students. Each was promoting the law school they were personally or professionally invested in.

After the presentations, the crowd of approximately 100 prospective students was given an opportunity to question the panel. The topic shifted very quickly to admissions and quotas. Each university responded with their institutional message for diversity and inclusion and was happy with their representation of women and minorities in their student body.

Then something very exciting happened. An American student of African or Hispanic ethnicity stood up and asked the most remarkable and insightful question about racial insecurity and higher education. "So what are white people going to think?" He asked, slipping out of his professional guise and showing his vulnerability.

He couldn't have been more than twenty-one, and clearly concerned with proving his worthiness—not to attend law school, that was already proven by his invitation to attend—what he wanted to know was would he be able to prove his worthiness to people who might doubt his effort and his worth.

After a brief pause, one panelist, a new dean of admissions, dared to respond. She said, "Who cares what white people think?"

I almost fell out of my seat. It was brash, blunt, and to the point. Not surprisingly the room fell silent. I thought, "How can I be as confident as this woman?"

After a brief pause, she continued.

"If you are making decisions about the most important thing in your life based on what one race of people, one group of people, or one person thinks about you, you are not only ill-prepared for law, you are ill-prepared for life."

I was blown away. I was a fan.

"You must prepare yourself and let the chips fall where they may," she continued. "If opportunity comes across your path, by all means take it as generations of people of all backgrounds and situations have done before you and will continue to do after you. Now, this is your moment."

Her words would influence the rest of my life and the choices about who I give my personal power too, if at all. She was making clear that our first responsibility was to represent our authentic self and our best selves.

She went on to ask us to keep two things in mind. First, that life is not about what other people think, but about preparation and timing. Second, it is also about realizing that when we succumb or subvert our entire life based on what other people think, we relinquish control to individuals we usually don't know well enough to see us through to the end.

It was an answer young decision makers with the weight of others on their shoulders should hear. Another person's opinion should not be the foundation we base our decisions on. It is only when you free your life from the weight of other people's opinions that you really get to know yourself.

How did she get there? I wondered. How did she figure it out without the clutter of indecision and lack of self-confidence so many of us always have in the background influencing the choices we make? I learned that day that we must first start by listening to our inner voice. Only you know what direction is best for your life.

Declutter your mind, remove the fear, believe in your self-worth, and divest yourself of insecurities based on other people's opinions. Only then will you be able to hear and be your true self.

When you reach the end of what you should know, you will be at the beginning of what you should sense."
—Kahlil Gibran

How we can influence our brain's thinking pattern?

New brain research shows that the more an individual tells lies, the more likely their brain is to become accustomed to it and eventually shift these brain sensors to a neutral state where the lies no longer register as false to the person telling them. This state of delusion can result in self- sabotaging behaviors that have the potential to be harmful to everyone around us and derail our true path in life.

Admitting to living in a LifeSpace of delusion is one of the hardest realities to bear, but it saved Lacey's future happiness. It came with a life changing revelation. "Nice girls do tell lies." Not only do they tell lies frequently and often, they tell them to themselves as much as they tell them to others. She tells her story.

LACEY

I met Brett during his visit to Atlanta for a rock concert. We were both there with mutual friends and quickly hit it off after he accidentally spilled a drink on my head. He apologized profusely, bought me several drinks, a concert T-shirt, and couldn't do enough to express his apology. He looked absolutely horrified and embarrassed. I was immediately smitten with his sincerity and taken by his charm. Brett was an aerospace engineering student in Daytona. He was six years my senior and expected to graduate in two years.

Brett was born in Canada and lived in North Carolina with his American-born sister. His parents immigrated to the U.S. without him and his sister was born shortly thereafter. He arrived in New York when he was six and met her for the first time when she was three years old. As they became best friends, he spent his teenage years discovering the joys of growing up in New York City.

At the time, Brett was struggling with his relationship with his father. He was the oldest and the only son at twenty-two. He would be the first to attend college, but after a year of taking courses at a college in upstate New York, he dropped out and was now starting over in Daytona at a four-year university specializing in avionics. His proud French-Canadian father, who left when he was three, told him he was a failure. This was his second chance to get it right.

In the looks and charm department Brett was an A+. He spoke French and was extremely handsome, thoughtful, and sensitive. He wrote poems on napkins and mailed them to me. We started dating when I was in my second year at community college. I had plans to attend the local university.

In my junior year of business school, he fell in love with me. I was charmed and firmly fixated on growing into love but I wasn't there yet. I was plagued by uncertainly and doubt. He knew I was close enough for him to want to wait for me. There was no tangible or concrete reason not to love Brett. He was wonderful and my parents loved him.

Two years into my first career, Brett was still working to pay his college expenses and was struggling to finish. I knew that soon after his graduation he would propose. I then realized our career progression would be quite different. I was in no hurry for him to finish.

The reality was I had a secret and the closer we became, the more real was the secret.

It was nothing tangible or the kind that could be traced back to one terrible mistake. It was not that simple. I had an emotional secret and no matter how hard I tried to change it, it stuck with me and challenged me in every way.

I had been in love before and memories of it haunted me. Every comparison to Brett told me that our newfound relationship was full of fun, intrigue and affection, but not love. For me, love meant passion, and I did not yet feel it. But did I really need passion? Could our relationship work without it?

Brett was 6'0", lean and physically fit, with naturally curly brown hair. He was a runner and a swimmer. Exercising outdoors brought out his natural olive complexion. His perfect smile and sensual lips completed his handsome, chiseled face that made him look like a conqueror or an Indian warrior. Ken and Barbie was how my friends referred to us. We would have cute kids, I thought. But, the passion wasn't there and I wondered why.

Four years later, Brett was twenty-eight, completing his final semester and starting to wonder about our future. Questions about my lack of passion for him still plagued me, even when I wasn't looking for answers.

Good friends have way of making you face things you don't want to. My questions and doubts would soon come to a head during a visit from Cherise, one of my best friends. We were sitting on the patio of our favorite diner enjoying breakfast.

"I still don't know why you bought a house before getting married" Cherise said between mouthfuls of pancakes, butter and syrup. She was my best friend from high school. "I mean, shouldn't you wait? *He's* supposed to buy the house."

I had heard these gender rules over and over again. The 1940s mindset didn't fit into the reality of a modern woman. A woman who is making a good living for herself, and is capable of living on her own, and actively making daily decisions about her life. In some ways Brett expressed the same views about women and the order of things. He didn't say it openly because I was further into my career that he was in his. But, I knew he was biding the time when he felt he had more leverage. A job and a degree would surely change his position and his behavior would soon follow.

Cherise had known Brett since he and I first met. She was visiting from New Mexico. After graduation, she landed a job at an architectural design firm making nearly a third more than my salary as a loss prevention investigator. She hadn't compromised like so many of our friends. I was too afraid to turn down my first job offer and I was too proud or honest to continue looking once I had accepted. Cherise on the other hand, accepted at least two offers and then used the second to negotiate her salary for her current one. She even took out a student loan to pay for her moving expenses and a down payment on an apartment. For her it was all business.

"Companies do what is best for themselves daily," she would often tell me. "It's only fair that we approach it in the same way," she'd finish defiantly. She had a point.

I wondered why no one had given me this advice. I suppose it comes from parents who have been there. Mine were certainly not the corporate types. My father spent nearly thirty years at the same job. Though it made him proud, it made me sick. In contrast, five years was my limit to learn everything I need to know from an employer and the turning point to when I would start looking for other positions that needed my expertise.

This morning Cherise and I were enjoying each other's company and listening to the raindrops fall on the thatched roof of the café cabana. It was a year after I'd purchased a new four-bedroom, 2,000 square foot home. She reminded me of the Facebook chatter that emerged when I bought the house.

"Why would you buy a home without a husband?" Friends, family members, and co-workers all wanted to know.

I responded that it was my dowry and I was not going to put my life on hold for no good reason. I rationalized that if I were to get married we could either sell the house or move into it. Either way, it added value to my future. Being a homeowner also didn't tie me down in the least. Those arguments perpetuated a myth. Quite frankly, it liberated me, to seize the opportunity to invest in my future and to choose my home on my own terms.

Several of my single female friends had recently purchased their own home. There are moments few and far in between when your friends and even acquaintances say you inspired them or motivated them to make a decision that positively impacted their future. This was one of those decisions.

Cherise and I soon became lost in moments of memories encouraged between sips of mimosas. So, how is Ken, she asked? Her lips were pinched into a sassy smirk.

"You mean Brett," I replied.

"Yes, how is that sexy, Pan-American, French, West Indian God doing?"

"He's doing well. And I think he's going to propose soon," I confessed.

If I had learned anything about Brett, it was that his nature would tell him to have everything in order. But I wasn't happy anticipating his proposal, I was anxious.

"OMG! So how do you feel?"

I shrugged. "So, Brett and I will get married. I'll give him his son and we can get divorced in a couple of years."

My casual prediction of our future marriage and divorce caught me by surprise. Suppressed thoughts were freely flowing. The sight of a sorely missed friend who often knew more than she revealed gave way to a moment to exhale.

Somewhere these thoughts had been running, like an app in the back of my consciousness. My words hung in the air and floated above us unashamedly. It wasn't Cherise who was appalled, it was me. Not at my brashness, but at the feeling of exhalation I felt after having said them.

Cherise sat with her mimosa at her lips. Maybe she hadn't heard.

After a silent pause, she took in a long sip then put the glass on the table.

"So, I guess Ken and Barbie are breaking up." Cherise said in her usual straightforward way.

"Yes," I said matter-of-factly. "The perfect couple is not going to make it."

It was alternately ridiculous and fatalist. I was planning to marry, start a family and to divorce someone in one sitting. I now knew I needed to get out of it and move on. He would feel hurt and pain if I let it go on longer, and I would feel relief.

Relief was replacing shock. I smiled.

Cherise knew about my childhood sweetheart and confessed that she had always felt something was missing between Brett and I. She knew that when I purchased the house, it was a statement of something, but she didn't know what. I couldn't lie to her, to him or to myself anymore. I was afraid of being alone, but I couldn't ruin a future family and predict bringing pain into my unborn children's lives in order to feed that fear. I was prepared to end our relationship and live my life alone, if necessary.

We were over within a year. He had not completed his courses yet again and that was the final straw to move on. Brett's mother loved me too and she was anxious for her oldest and only son to start a family; she called me in tears. She deserved an explanation. They were in this relationship too. I felt horrible. I didn't want to hurt anyone or be thought of as a bad person.

I wanted to be nice, but I ended up cruel. I learned then that the need to satisfy everyone and wanting so desperately to be the good girl was a myth that had already ruined too many lives. I was willing to go to any length to be the nice, pleasant person I was expected to be. However, that was not my authentic self. It was self sabotaging my future happiness and I needed to listen to my inner thoughts.

Self-actualization starts with truth.

What is Your Choice?

To be smart is to know that self-delusion and self-denial lead to a shallow and gross misrepresentation of life. To be intelligent is to understand your own truth and to create a life that is actively engaged in pursuing what brings you joy and self-confidence that motivates you toward your true calling. (#DIVAauthenticself)

The person whose opinion you should value most is the person who has unlimited control over your life. That person is you. The path to intelligence starts with being authentic to yourself. It requires self-love, self-understanding, and respect for who you are becoming and will be. No one can change that unless you allow them to influence you and dictate your concerns. Activate, motivate and take charge of your authentic self.

Six Tips for Developing Mindfulness

Mindfulness is described as a state of active, open attention on the present. It is the practice of observing your thoughts, feelings and senses from an objective and open viewpoint, without judgment. Mindfulness means being present and engaged in the moment, not in the past or future. Instead of letting your life pass you by, connect with the energy of your present surroundings and awaken to the experience. Research shows that mindfulness helps us be more emotionally intelligent, more present, more creative, better able to make better decisions, better able to manage stress, and become more resilient.[xii]

1. Practice raising your self-awareness through active meditation for one minute a day. Start with simple breathing exercises to clear the head and lift the heart.

2. Allow yourself to experience your physical and mental presence in the moment by freeing the mind of judgment, inviting openness, and compassion for yourself and others.

3. Develop a personal mantra that you can draw upon for energy and affirmation. Incorporate it with or without meditation.

4. Practice visualization as part of your mediation. Visualizing something that calms you or soothes the mind will help to balance stressors and create broader meaning and awareness.
5. Download a mindfulness app or meditation music and incorporate it into your daily activities.
6. It is perfectly acceptable to practice mindfulness while you are in motion. You can incorporate mindfulness into walking by focusing on your presence in connection with the energy around you or by focusing on the rhythm of your breathing. I enjoy being mindful to the feeling of the sun on my skin, its energy, my energy and the sensation of that unique connection in the present moment. At the end, I feel aware, alive and very connected to my presence in the world.

Dr. V. Brooks Dunbar, D.M.

MASLOW'S HIERARCHY OF NEEDS

Maslow's Hierarchy of Needs[xiii] is one of the most referenced models for studying workforce motivation and theories of human motivation. Psychologist Abraham Maslow put forth the notion that we must fulfill our basic needs before we can move on to fulfilling broader needs. The model initially included five needs but has evolved to include a sixth and higher level of need to reflect individuals who sought to "identify with something greater than the individual self," he named this higher motivational level above self-actualization as "self-transcendence."[xiv]

Motivational Level	Human Need
Self-transcendence	Seeks to further a cause beyond the self and ego: service to a cause or others, divine, spiritual, transpersonal experiences, communion with others or universal ideals, peak experience that transcends beyond personal self.
Self-actualization	Seeks personal fulfillment: awareness, honesty, freedom, trust
Esteem	Seeks esteem: respect, confidence, recognition and achievement
Love/Belonging	Seeks group affiliation and affinity: friendship, family, intimacy
Safety	Seeks security through law and order: self, family, health, property, and employment
Physiological	Seeks basic necessities of life: breathing, eating, drinking, sleeping

Many coaching practices today, mine included, use tools and methods that are informed by Positive Psychology. This new approach to holistic health explores behavior and mental wellness through our strengths and level of satisfaction with life. The University of Pennsylvania's Authentic Happiness website is loaded with self tests or questionnaires to help individuals determine what truly makes them happy and how this affects well-being. The below link will take you directly to a broad list of questionnaires organized in categories of emotion, engagement, flourishing, life satisfaction, and meaning. I chose to take the Values in Action (VIA) questionnaire, which is listed in the engagement category, to assess what 24 values are natural to me and which I must put forth greater effort to project. The five values that were most natural to me are fairness, kindness, hope, perspective, and perseverance. I pride myself in being a curious person and that trait was number six. The values I have to make a conscious effort to work towards include spirituality, humility, leadership, social intelligence, and self-regulation. I couldn't help but think that the last value has more to do with my increasing awareness of my inability to maintain a healthy diet over extended periods of time. Each report explains how to interpret the results and how the value is defined for that specific survey. You must register to take any questionnaire. The link to the Authentic Happiness home page is: https://www.authentichappiness.sas.upenn.edu

Career

Noun: an occupation undertaken for a significant period of a person's life and with opportunities for progress.

Synonyms: profession, occupation, job, vocation, calling, employment, line of work, walk of life, métier.

Our career refers to our professional work or life work or life's calling. It encompasses our occupation, current employment or profession within an industry or sector or across multiple industries. It refers to the drive to answer our calling in life and the ability to transform to acquire the lifestyle we want to live.

7

OWN YOUR PERSONA, MANAGE IT WELL

"Life isn't about finding yourself. Life is about creating yourself." – George Bernard Shaw

Beverly is a thirty-five-year-old sales director and event planner from Atlanta. She is a petite and charming southern belle with an infectious accent. Now entering her third career, she found herself in a new role that challenged her to work with individuals born in different generations. She wanted coaching to help manage team conflict that was affecting her performance on the job.

A key measure of intelligence is the ability to manage personality while displaying sound character. The earlier you develop these traits and learn to understand them, the better your opportunities for success. Research associated with positive psychology suggests that personality is a core trait that remains relatively stable over time; therefore, a person who is operating from a position of what they are naturally good at, their talent, is operating from a position of strength and is more likely to be successful.[xv] Personality therefore is the driver of how we use our intelligence in more effective ways that lead to success.

Your persona helps you to have personal power and authority over yourself and others. It is natural to perceive then, that if your persona is that of a shy and withdrawn individual, this perception will drive your social and professional life, and influence your private relationships. Understanding your soft skills and knowing your strengths and weaknesses will help you to manage your persona and your influence over others. The benefit in the workplace is that it allows you to minimize self-sacrifice made from bad decisions or working on teams that may not be the best fit for you. It certainly improves performance in our everyday lives.

As a self-management skill, your persona gives you the power and authority to navigate your life. It is the tool that allows us to survive in difficult situations and to meet our personal needs. It also dictates who we invite into our lives and who we repel.

The ability to manage your persona is a leadership trait that is associated with the power to influence others. In life, that power is associated with personal power which also transfers into organizations.

BEVERLY

"If this is the time to talk about my worst employee ever, then let's get it over with because I don't have the energy it deserves to put into it," Beverly said, as she waited for our interview to start.

Five years ago, Rosalyn, Beverly's worst employee, left for a new job and she was still experiencing a strong emotional reaction whenever she thought of her. Beverly knew, without a doubt, that Rosalyn was a younger version of herself. If she could find all of her old bosses, she would apologize and refund them the therapy they surely endured at her hands. Her hard lesson on the professional value of social and emotional intelligence came at a cost and it was priceless.

What Beverly was passionately reflecting on was her first hard lesson on the critical difference in leading either a successful or dysfunctional team. Firmly set in the middle of her young career, she was facing a team made up of individual personalities that collectively and individually lacked crucial human and social skills. This deficit manifested in behaviors that reflected a deficiency in the kind of intelligent thinking that would lead to good decision making and problem solving.

It's now five years later and Beverly is still visibly moved by her experience. She starts our interview by recalling her very first team meeting. She had been notified of her selection for the position and before her official start date, their supervisor had arranged for Beverly to have a lunch meeting to meet the team. The meet-and-greet with the new boss was their idea.

Rosalyn was in her early twenties, five foot three inches tall and all of a size zero, if I had to guess. Her hair was brown in a shoulder length, bone-straight cut with messy bangs pushed off to the side of one brow. Her brown eyes twinkled with interest while a fixed smile gave away the enormous energy it took to sustain such a feat of sincerity. She sat quietly and offered her hand when her turn came to introduce herself. Only then did her smile become more relaxed, and suggestive of an even temperament. She sat farthest into the booth with her back against the pony wall. It appeared this gave her a sense of ownership of the occasion. I knew instantly she was going to be trouble.

Cynthia, who sat opposite Rosalyn, was clearly in her late thirties with bleached blonde hair and press-on nails. She leaned forward in the booth with her elbows on the table as though eagerly anticipating what was to come. It was clear these two had led the charge to meet and greet me as their new boss. I imagined they had a hand in the previous director's departure, and it was clear they were there to size me up.

Cynthia was friendly and the first to speak. She was experienced and had the longest tenure and had seen many bosses come and go. She offered the appropriate level of cordiality to fit the occasion. I had already read their résumés.

Mark was sitting on the outer edge of the booth. He smiled as though happy just to be out of the office and made several courteous gestures. There was nothing pretentious or exceptional about him outside of his boyish charm and fit physique. I could tell he simply wanted to work and enjoy himself. He wanted freedom to be creative and nothing more.

As work settled in, personalities began to unfold. The office is a Petri dish for lessons in why some succeed in their job while others excel. It's simply a matter of intelligence over smarts. I didn't know how to teach that.

Although she was the youngest and newest member of the group, Rosalyn was clearly the most educated. She had a bachelor's degree while Cynthia and Mark had two years of technical training. She also spoke Spanish, although not fluently, and was a member of a college business program that matched college graduates with company internships, fellowships and training.

Her Midwest upbringing was influenced by Catholicism and its spirituality that informed select behaviors she prioritized for herself and others. Part of that orderly worldview included a strict sense to detail and adherence to rules. Work questions were answered by days of investigation and detailed responses. She took pride in her ability to accomplish tasks and to deliver them free of error. This clearly empowered her, as did her need to ask for additional meetings to clarify work assignments and specific duties. Her skills at answering the phones were sharp and well rehearsed. Her ability to multi-task, pay attention to detail, and follow through were exceptional.

In contrast to her task management, Rosalyn perceived individuals as tasks that should be ordered and rule-based. There was little comprehension for alternative forms of thoughts or behaviors outside of those spiritually inspired and Midwest values. No one was spared, not even the executive office who received constant visits from her to express how work was not being performed according to her perception of the employment codes and performance measures their leadership team had set.

My boss made it clear to me, "We do not have time for it." I was on notice to better manage my team member.

A test of her imposed and compartmentalized thinking came to a standoff than during our festival planning.

"Rosalyn, I need you to sit in on the upcoming planning meeting for the Summer Festival and report back on what is expected of us." I told her.

She replied as expected. "Yes, but what do you want me to do?"

We were the lead team for a regional Fourth of July festival, which drew annually more than 20,000 visitors. Because of the current recession, the festival committee was concerned that we could fall short of sponsorship goals and ticket sales. Our responsibility was to cross-promote the event, share marketing and publicity costs, secure sponsors, and provide our equipment and personnel. We were in the hot seat because we were behind in sponsorships and publicity.

Sponsorships were Rosalyn's responsibility and although we understood her dilemma, we still had to report and explain our challenges.

Rosalyn saw the request as a personal attack. She thought my request for her to attend the meeting was an effort to make her look foolish.

I continued, "Our contact is Rafael, I'll have a separate meeting with him, but I need to trust you to take detailed notes so that I can have a clear account of the discussions from the other members of the planning committee."

I knew this would be a challenge for her; she didn't always work well with interaction of any kind. There always seemed to be territorial issues confounded by attention seeking and poor self-management.

Despite these concerns, the team needed her to step up to her responsibilities. We had recently lost a key member of the team and everyone had taken on more work.

As the time for the festival approached, Rosalyn's constant questions and awkwardness made me wonder if putting her in charge of the assignment had been a good idea. However, this test of her abilities to lead a project was necessary. My concern was that she would fall apart before the event. Of course she did, several times and each time I handled the situation or brought in reinforcements. I always had a Plan B and a supportive colleague on standby and these private conversations and sidebar negotiations made all the difference in things going from bad, to worse, to irreparable. Keep these types of colleagues around you. They are invaluable and will determine the outcome of your success. They will also vouch for your work behind the scene.

The final straw happened the day before the event. I would characterize the mood of the team at that time as stressed but upbeat. The festival was something we were all looking forward to. Part of our responsibility with publicity was not only to provide graphics support, but also hardware. In past years, this had been pushed off to an outside vendor and the costs absorbed by a partner.

On the day before the event, there was a discrepancy about who was coordinating pick-up and delivery to the festival location. It is the responsibility of the hiring firm to hire the truck to pick up and drop off hardware to and from the location. During the last committee meeting two days prior, Rosalyn had told the committee that we would pick up and deliver the hardware in addition to purchasing a few additional units and paying for it. This opened us up to a tremendous amount of liability exposure for our staff.

I brought this to Rosalyn's attention during our final pre-event team meeting.

"Rosalyn, we're not accepting the liability for transporting the equipment. And our team is not going to be open to the potential of physical injury from picking up such heavy equipment. Surely you've noticed how heavy the equipment is?"

"Well how is this going to make me look?" she asked. She could barely contain her anger and frustration at what she thought was a criticism of her leadership ability.

"I can assure you Rosalyn," I replied, "they are not concerned how you look. They are concerned with completing the job."

What this smart employee hadn't yet realized was that leadership and authority reached far beyond her and her position.

At some point, I became concerned with her mental and physical well-being. I knew I needed outside help. I felt there was something wrong with Rosalyn and I wasn't sure if it was external of the office or internal. Her fits of anger and outbursts at anyone she felt was encroaching on her space and position was concerning.

It was affecting other teams and departments. I found myself apologizing to coworkers she had been rude too or had criticized, because they had disagreed with her even slightly. I began to look for signs of domestic violence, anger management issues and personality disorder. I called our employee assistance program, which provided support for extended families. I asked if they provided professional development training on teamwork. Fortunately, they were certified to provide individual and group dynamics training, and I immediately scheduled a workshop for my team.

The results were invaluable. The personal assessments matched our personalities and behavioral tendencies perfectly. For Rosalyn, it illustrated a personality type that needed order, was highly judgmental, felt threatened by authority, and that was comfortable working alone. In other words, Rosalyn felt she did not need supervision.

After reviewing the reports and accepting the trainers' recommendations, I then began to play to her needs that I could manage, but it did not address the anger management problems. It was enough to buy time, but I secretly started to look for another job for her. She was best working in an office alone, without others around her. Her technical skills were excellent, but her personality skills were dismal and they put the reputation of the department at risk.

Hire character. Train skill." – Peter Schultz

A Lesson on the Power of Personality and Success in Organizations

Beverly's experience with Rosalyn taught her a lot about leadership and the power of personality to make or destroy an organization.

Many cases show that that personal power can be more valuable than position power. Presidential elections often reflect this kind of personal and charismatic power to influence and motivate others versus their ability to be successful in a position—where power that is attached to the role or title and not the person. Personal power follows you and gets more refined over time. It is the combination of your character and personality that adds value to the power that comes with the position or title. It is what draws people to you or pushes them away from you.

Possession of a role or title does not automatically equate to leadership. For example, a person in a leadership role that was assigned to them may not possess leadership ability. The position that comes with formal authority can also come with resources and incentives that can be used to motivate and influence others. The ability to offer bonuses and time off is an example of an incentive that comes with a leadership position. However, these are not dependent on the presence of leadership ability or personal power, but it does influence the leader's ability to be effective and the degree to which they can be successful at work.

Personality is a powerful leadership talent that can be developed into a powerful leadership skill. A leadership skill is "the ability to use one's knowledge and competences to accomplish a set of goals and outcomes."[xvi] It's a game changer.

Our persona is what we choose to display to others, our personality is who we really are—our authentic self or our inner self. The capacity to develop intelligence is a leadership skill that can be effective in producing success. Intelligence is achieved in two ways, what we are generally born with and what comes from learning as we mature. How much we maximize and develop our capacity to utilize intelligence to inform our thinking and resulting behavior is completely within our control. Our personality dictates how these traits are applied and displayed.

Our human and social skill is one of the three leadership skills than can be self-developed. In some cases our technical skills can be self-developed as well. As you start on your personal, professional and career journey, the ability to create and sustain relationships is the most important work experience you will attain that keeps you relevant. As you go higher up on the corporate ladder, you'll notice that corporate investment in personality assessments will surpass technical skills assessments.

I do believe that people at work don't really care who we are, they care about what they need us to be. It's part of the service we are expected and required to deliver for the fulfillment of the job. When your personality isn't a fit for success, develop the persona that is.

Simplified, your persona is your social self rather than your inner self (the authentic self). Understanding the relationship between the two is paramount to build your social paradigm and create social networks whether online, perceived, or real, that contribute to your ability to successfully meet the complex situations that present themselves in your life.

The Big Five Personality Assessment

Personality is the main ingredient for social intelligence; it is directly associated with leadership effectiveness and is one of the three individual attributes of leadership, the other two being motivation and drive.[xvii] The importance of developing social intelligence cannot be understated. Organizations spend billions annually on employee training and development designed to help individuals utilize their inherent traits more effectively to improve performance.

The Big Five Personality Assessments are one of the most popular workplace assessments. It measures what are believed to be the five major dimensions of human personality:

- introversion/extraversion
- disorganized/conscientious
- disagreeable/agreeable
- closed-minded/open-minded
- calm-relaxed /nervous-high-strung.

These assessments measure an individual's tendencies toward certain personality behaviors when compared with a larger sample of individuals who have taken the assessment.

Opportunities to improve traits include participation in leadership development programs that assess leadership skills and inventory traits. Like most assessments, these personality measures consist of multiple questions that are phrased to force a natural response for which most closely describes you or your behavior. The answers are then coded to correspond with a personality type.

Below is an example of The Big Five Personality Assessment using my results compared against my husband's results on a scale of 0 to 100 percent. For example, I tend to lean toward introversion at 27 percent, while my husband is on the opposite end of the scale which is more extraverted at 83 percent. I scored high in open-mindedness at 70 percent, while my husband leans toward a more closed-minded end of the scale at 12 percent.

Big Five Personality Traits MY ASSESSMENT SCORES	My Scores/My Spouse's Scores*
• Introverted/Extraverted • Calm, Relaxed/Nervous, High-Strung • Disorganized/Conscientious • Disagreeable/Agreeable • Closed-Minded/Open-Minded	27/83 2/9 96/74 79/87 70/12
A link to the assessment may be found at: *http://www.outofservice.com/bigfive/*	*Note: I completed my spouses' assessment for him.*

The results of these assessments can then inform behaviors. For example, my results from The Big Five Personality Dimension[xviii] assessment revealed that my dominant personality trait leans toward introversion. Wanting to improve on my introvert tendencies, I focused on developing extroverted behaviors. However, when placed in a work environment that required extroversion, I was able to deliberately engage in more social behaviors and self-monitor when my natural tendency for introversion was becoming more dominant.

As a fundraising director, part of my job was to plan fundraising events, solicit donors, and write grant proposals. My strength was in writing, after all I was a journalism major, but my weakness was in proactively engaging others—that required more talking in support of my fundraising. As a natural introvert, my goal was to increase my social connections by proactively engaging individuals. I attended more professional and social activities. Subsequently my fundraising increased. Years later, I took the assessment again and my scores indicated that I was an extrovert. Most recently after taking the assessment for the third time, I had reverted back to my natural tendencies of being an introvert. I took two separate assessments and scored 50% on one and 27% on the other. Because my career had changed, I was no longer motivated to be an extrovert, and my natural inclination took over.

More importantly, what the assessments revealed is that I had the ability to manage my introversion to meet my personal and career goals when needed.

Additional training and development activities that identify individual characteristics such as strengths and weaknesses, also support knowledge acquisition, professional development, and increase confidence in decision making. Activities like leadership coaching, shadowing, and goal setting also helped to manage and/or improve traits. Although my natural traits are still dominant, I have the ability to temporarily adopt behaviors to mimic desired traits, and in few cases sustain the change.

I encourage you to go to the source sites listed in the reference pages at the back of this book or Google "personality assessments" and use them to inform you of your own natural tendencies. While these are very helpful self-development tools, it's important to understand that these assessments are used to help you identify your range of traits and develop opportunities for improvement in areas where you are challenged.

For my own leadership development, I also completed an assessment that measures personality across sixteen dimensions. The assessment somewhat confirmed what previous assessments indicated, that I was at times, perceived as "cold." Fortunately, this perception can be improved through professional development, education, and training. For example, "warmth" according to Cattell's 16 Personality Factors,[xix] is associated with being supportive and comforting versus cold and selfish. This people skill may indicate a person's ability to be empathetic. I have often rated in the mid range of these scores and have worked very hard to appear to be more open, to listen more intently, and to be less judgmental. Communication has been the single factor that has positively shifted coworker's perceptions of me from being cold and more task-oriented to having an inviting, open, and engaged demeanor. I also found that this correlated with my degree of social intelligence, which also improved because I was better able to relate to others. The full descriptions of Cattell's 16 Personality Factors is shown below.

FINDING YOUR PERSONALITY STRENGTHS AND WEAKNESSES

Cattell's 16 Personality Factors Test is a free online assessment that helps you to assess your dominant personality types. Personality is proven to remain constant throughout our lives (Rath, 2007), however, our persona reflects the ability to self-manage our areas of strength as well as areas in which we are challenged.

The below table represents an example of Cattell's 16 Factor Key for Personality Types. It lists my assessment scores on a range of 0 to 100 percent to reflect the percentage of what personality trait we are more likely to naturally exhibit. What stands out for me is that I scored 14 on the sensitivity scale. It suggests that I may need to work on my level of sensitivity to the environment or toward others. When I consider this score in comparison with other assessments, this holistic view can be associated with my level of introversion, which I'm happy to see is my highest score ever at 50 percent.

Cattell's 16 Factor Key for Personality Types *MY ASSESSMENT SCORES*	
Warmth	42
Intellect	86
Emotional Stability	74
Aggressiveness	42
Liveliness	42
Dutifulness	38
Social Assertiveness	70
Sensitivity	14
Paranoia	30
Abstractness	22
Introversion	50
Anxiety	10
Open-mindedness	74
Independence	54
Perfectionism	46
Tension	58
A link to the assessment may be found at: personality-testing.info/tests/16PF.php	

The more aware you are of your innate or authentic personality, the more empowered you are to self-direct your own training and professional development to reach your life and career goals. Don't wait to be selected for professional development at work. Trust me, if you've already left a bad impression, you are likely to be the last selected for leadership development training. Self-select yourself to improve your life skills in all areas. That begins now.

*When Your Personality is Your Achilles Heel,
Adopt One that Works*

This story is one told by a personal friend, we'll call her Sam, with whom I've had many conversations that led to personal, pro-bono coaching. She tells of her struggle with trying to adopt a more outgoing personality and the first time this was brought to her attention at a sorority pledge event.

SAM

As a freshman in college, I had developed a persona which, one could argue, equaled my personality.

People who interacted with me encountered a raw, unfiltered personality molded by my parents insistence on teaching me that "telling the truth was always better than not." Unlike me, my common-sense sister did not blindly accept that rule. Instead, she practiced the inconsequential "I don't know anything" approach.

Although I had no self-awareness or concept of my personality, people around me seemed put off or intimidated by my words and behavior. I gave no thought to this because I was satisfied with my small group of friends, two to be exact. We were members of an official little-sister group who made up the volunteer corps of a campus fraternity. This was a popular way for the fraternities to expand their volunteer base by establishing a little sister auxiliary. It became so popular that the sororities started creating their own volunteer corps that were made up of all men. Out of this group of ten women who were all college freshmen, the three of us seemed to have the same nonjudgmental and easy going personality. I later found out that I was considered more "nonchalant" than nonjudgmental, and in the workplace, there was a big difference in not caring versus withholding opinion.

I would discover that difference after I decided to join a sorority. It was girls' night out with my pledge class. Girls' night out was an occasion for the sorority members to take turns challenging you on any aspect of your personality, behavior or personal topic they chose. The objective, I later realized, was to get you to identify your personality flaws or weaknesses and to get you to push through them. The intent was to make you mentally stronger. Tonight was our "breakdown" session with the big sisters. The session started after dinner, which we prepared, and lasted well into the early morning hours. The big sisters laughed, made fun of, and mimicked us. I wondered if they had classes the next morning. After all, it was a weeknight.

There were six of us pledges and an equal number of big sisters who were in their junior or senior year with one in graduate school. We were placed in circles and each pledge was asked to say something negative and something positive about the other members of the circle. This was to determine if we had the character and temperament to become full members of the sorority. In retrospect, this was clearly my first structured interview although the feelings of intimidation, anxiety and fear made it feel more chaotic.

There would be many more to follow. But this instigation and interrogation between pledges and our observers proved invaluable.

At the end of it all, I learned for the first time that I was perceived to be a realist, cold toward others, and nonchalant in my demeanor and about matters of importance to other people. In the positive critique, I was perceived as thoughtful, considerate and dependable.

It was the first time I realized that how people perceived me, greatly impacted my capacity to engage others. It dictated my friendships when someone else's perceptions of me kept me out of certain activities, organizations, and circles of influence. I was just beginning to acquire the knowledge to engage my social intelligence skills so that I could manage my behaviors to have more effective and successful relationships.

What I realized was that my proven leadership traits had positioned me to be successful in winning student office positions. But I stalled when it came to making the important social connections needed to move up the ladder of achieving greater influence and success. As the saying goes, I had peaked. That night was the beginning of my self-awareness and self-development.

During a time when sororities and fraternities are associated with severe hazing, partying, drinking, and engaging in other excesses, the experience helped me on my path to gaining social intelligence. As my self-awareness evolved, even more surprising was how young men also participated in advancing those limiting perceptions by passing on misconceptions and putting false characterizations out there regardless of whether they knew you personally or not.

When listening to others and measuring yourself against online assessments or otherwise, remember to say to yourself, out loud if needed, *"Someone else's opinion of me will never be the basis of my entire being."* We have inherent skills and traits that are uniquely ours. People who don't have them may not understand them and may question your application of them to meet the requirements of work and life situations. Take charge of who you are as a person. Get to know yourself better. Then let it breathe and live in you, be mindful of it. Own it. Manage it. Live it. This is called happiness.

What is Your Choice?

To be smart is to know that life is an opportunity to display your talent and be successful. Intelligence understands that life is a social construct. No matter how essential your skills and abilities; personality and character will dictate the opportunities offered to you and the time it takes to achieve a higher-level of success. If your personality traits make it achievable at all. (#DIVAownyourpersona)

There is no mistaking the fact that personality can help, hurt, or hold you back in life and career. The gift of an engaging and attractive personality is something that is a natural trait for a fraction of the population. If you were not born with this trait, or complimentary traits that offset your tendency towards opposite degrees of the spectrum, then develop a persona that turns your weaknesses into a strength. Regardless of your true personality, you can create a persona that supports your goals. Take ownership and responsibility of it. It's your path to success.

Five Tips to Develop Your Persona

1. Take a personality assessment to identify your personality strengths and potential weaknesses.
2. Ask trusted friends, family members and co-workers to list five personality traits that compliment you and five personality traits that may hinder you.

3. Think about the persona want to portray and the skills required to adopt the behaviors that align with this personality.
4. Create a personal or leadership development plan with action steps to attain your specific goals and also to see how these strengths and weaknesses fit into the leadership development plan. An example of a leadership development plan, The Leadership Self-Inventory, is included at the end of Chapter 18.
5. Actively practice and manage the behaviors that will help you to achieve your goal.

8
YES, PRETTY IS A TALENT… USE IT WISELY

"Never downplay your intelligence. Dumb is not cute. Integrity, dignity, and wisdom are the true indicators of beauty." — *Unknown*

Deanna is a forty-two-year-old sales rep from Richmond. She is an attractive 5' 9" brunette; a classic beauty with striking features. She felt she was being overlooked for promotions despite being a top performer. She wanted coaching to improve her relationships at work and to better understand what was holding back her career. When she finally reached that place of self-realization, Deanna meets Jannie, a coworker, whose workplace behavior brings further clarity on how her past behavior may have led to her unknowingly turning away past mentorship and leadership opportunities. This story illustrates the harm of limited perception and insular thinking, and the importance of

developing a heightened self-awareness to create effective relationships at work.

"Don't waste the pretty." That is a quote from a successful businessman and very public figure in my adopted home state. Everyone knows his name. It was said to a friend of mine during a private conversation where he was attempting to give her sound professional advice on how to turn around her small fledging real estate business. It could have been interpreted in many ways, but without being in the room, you wouldn't have known that he was speaking to her like a father to a daughter. He had, after all, five sons and no daughters. This was clearly a moment of genuine reflection and consideration for what he believed a young woman and sole proprictor would have to acknowledge and address if she wanted to be successful. His crass and reality-based assessment of the female businesswoman was simple. It would be naïve to overlook the most obvious thing that will both help and hinder your path to success. That's the elephant in the room.

Let's be very clear, appearance matters, looks matter, and attitude matters. Not singularly, but collectively they must all work together if you want to influence people or draw them to you. Within this perspective is the importance of motivation and how fear affects our ability to assert ourselves in both the most routine and the most critical decision-making moments of our lives. This may come as a surprise but among the list of top ten fears is the fear of talking to people of the opposite sex. I believe this anxiety stems from a fear of rejection and failure. There are numerous cases when a person is highly self-aware of their attractiveness and wield it to dominate, intimidate and control others.

This was the case with Deanna who was often told that she could be a model. She enjoyed hearing this and also the sense of attention and distraction she invoked in others. Eventually, she began to adopt what she believed to be the mindset, style and attitude she believed came with that role. Unfortunately, she was a member of the blue-suit industry and not the fashion industry. She was a field sales representative for a pharmaceutical company.

Deanna's example of how attractiveness and personality can derail success in career and life is a classic tale because it contradicts the myth that parents, counselors, mentors and teachers tell us to motivate us to excel. "You can be anything you want as long as you study hard and get an education," they would say. What I've found is that intelligence and personality have more of an influence on success, while fear influences motivation or how far you are willing to go.

Although beautiful, her beauty was only skin deep. Not only was Deanna critical, she didn't hide it. She could be so annoying that few people took the time to tell her that her behavior was a turn off. Because of her looks she was always among the first to be considered when the company needed a representative. What she didn't know, was that she was also the first to be considered among the list of who should not be considered. She never quite understood why other employees always seemed to get an extra nudge on the job. She had excellent performance reviews. Was the top performer two years in a row, and was usually the first to step up and volunteer for opportunities to lead training and development programs. In contrast, she saw the employees who were chosen for extra attention, as meek and passive. Point by point she felt she out performed and out hustled them all.

Today was another one of those days. Deanna arrived at work to a flurry of excitement. After a successful five years of steady growth, the owners announced the company was looking to expand into

Dallas and they would need a key team of managers to lead this effort. Team members interested in moving were asked to enter their names into a job pool for consideration.

Deanna was mobile. She was a newlywed and she and her husband were looking to move out of the rural south to a more diverse and culturally progressive community to start a family. That morning was particularly exciting because the decisions had been made. At noon, the team of twenty gathered in the conference room to hear the results by video teleconference. The announcement was quick and the celebration even quicker. Two men and two women would relocate to open the new office. Deanna was not one of them. Not only was she not chosen, they decided to go with two individuals who had less seniority. That was the last straw. That was the fourth time she felt slighted by her boss. Why hadn't he gone to bat for her? She decided to ask him.

DEANNA

"Looking back, I was very rude and abrasive in that meeting." Deanna said with a smile and a voice that oozed both confidence and all the certainty of a woman who knew exactly what she was doing, who she was, and how she needed to do it. That memorable meeting was six years ago and the firm was now a distant, but life-learning memory.

"My boss said very little at the beginning, he even agreed that I may have been overlooked and he would make the effort to include me in more opportunities." She said with a sigh. "Unfortunately, I'd made up my mind that there would be no more opportunities with that company. I was out. But I needed to know why they'd made it so hard."

Deanna, now a mom of two, didn't look more than thirty; however, her resume placed her in her early forties which matched her confidence and style. Her hair and makeup were perfectly done, almost too perfect, down to the black penciled in mole that sat atop her brow. She resembled a brunette sex symbol from the 70's, like Sophia Loren, Joan Collins, and Lauren Bacall. She didn't have the insecurities of many career-driven women burdened with guilt from a working marriage and free-range kids in tow.

Deanna recalled the meeting lasted for more than an hour. Her boss wanted to say something, but he was hesitant. So, she provoked him.

"I intimidate you don't I?"

He smiled and looked at his shoes, scrutinized the pattern on his tie. When he looked up his demeanor changed. His face had a look of power, the power that comes from knowing what others really think of you and the outcomes of your immediate future. Dan was about the same age as Deanna, but he had the respect of leadership and those closest to him. He arrived early each day and like Deanna, was driven. Although they didn't speak much at work, they greeted each other warmly both inside and outside of work. He was a nice guy, a professional, and his above average performance was to be expected.

But that day, Dan decided in that moment to let go any concern for office politics, political correctness or administrative policy. He would go to that place of no return.

"Actually the issue is that your attitude is poor and people hate working with you," he said matter-of-factly.

I looked at him in a puzzled and shocked expression. The horrifying reality was that I had no idea what he meant by that. Just as quickly as he opened the door for me to challenge him, he closed it in my shocked face. He offered nothing more.

I left the company, and the interesting thing was I still had that monkey on my back. No one ever came up to me and taught me the value of attitude over looks, intelligence, experience, and even knowledge. None of that matters if people just don't want to work with you and they certainly aren't going to recommend you to their friends. How would they defend that sort of personality?

"I've always been told I'm pretty, but I came to realize I also have an attitude problem," Deanna admitted. "It's something I wasn't aware of. I'm a perfectionist and have been known to be too skeptical or critical even to this day."

> *"No matter how plain a woman may be, if truth and honesty are written across her face, she will be beautiful."* — *Eleanor Roosevelt*

My "aha" moment came interestingly enough after I left the company for a management position with a new firm. I supervised a small satellite office of twelve employees who ranged in age and gender. They had all been there for several years before I came onboard with the exception of Jannie, a new employee who was hired just three months earlier.

Jannie's behavior toward me illustrated what kind of nightmare I must have been. She was about average in the looks and brains department, but her disposition toward me was awful. She didn't have any problems with her peers; however, she clearly had a problem with authority. That was evident from our first introduction. Some people are cordial and extend the courtesy of a smile with a handshake. On the other hand, she simply studied my face for some sort of giveaway expression she could manipulate. Somewhere in her mind a Rolodex of thoughts was turning. She was trying really hard to figure me out.

It started immediately. Within the first week, the phones rang and she did not answer them. Instead, another employee rushed to answer the call. Jannie then walked over to me and decided to instruct me on answering the phones. Small tests of my authority continued. When I asked her to do a task and she replied that she was busy. Our office was seasonally busy and this was not a busy season.

I eventually called in personality test experts to help the team understand each other's personalities. Sure enough, Jannie was a perfectionist, a dreamer who thought the world was only as she saw it.

As my boss before me, I gave her great evaluations. She excelled at her job; however, I'd also listen and watch how she spoke to clients in a brash, matter-of-fact, and argumentative tone. I initially wanted to get her some help and advice, but I knew that she would not take it well. After discovering she was requesting meetings with my boss to discuss my decisions, I decided that although she clearly needed a mentor, I could not give her any advice. Her behavior was such a turn off, that I would be wasting my wisdom and expertise. I resolved to focus on the other members of the team. It was unfortunate because she could have learned a lot from my experiences. Like me, her wake-up call would come many years later and after many lost opportunities.

Leverage Attractiveness And Exercise Talent

"Pretty" plays a big role, if not the main role in some positions, when it comes to getting into the company and having opportunities handed to you. Training and education do matter; but, if there is the hint of hope that the pretty girl is capable of learning or acquiring the proper credentials, she will be given the benefit of the doubt. However, the combination of personality and social skills will determine how far she will go. Take advantage of "the pretty" because it adds value. But not even beauty will help people who are unpleasant to be around.

Companies hire for skill and fire for emotional intelligence. Attractiveness will give you the edge, but it won't save you if you're emotionally and socially inept.

What is Your Choice?

Smart is knowing that beauty is a resource and can open doors in the workplace. Intelligence is understanding that individuals lead with the head, the heart, and hand. Appearance is a resource that should be managed well. If it is not, no one will be able to save you, not even skill and competence. (#DIVAprettyisatalent)

The reality of physical attraction and outward appearance is a powerful resource to open doors and form new relationships. Use it wisely, carefully and with full understanding that ultimately your skill and competence will determine personal and professional success. Also be aware of what your unconscious personality is portraying to others. Lack of awareness of facial expressions such as rolling eyes, winks and smirks and non-verbal body cues such as crossed arms are a few unconscious messages that can sabotage your progression in life.

Six Tips for Managing the Problem/Gift of Being Attractive:

1. Keep it in perspective. Bet on your talent and skills, which appreciate in value. Attraction in the workplace and in careers depreciates and can only take you so far.

2. Use attractiveness in the same manner as any other skill or trait. If someone compliments your beauty, respond as they have complimented your work and use the subject of work to shift the conversation to business.

3. Be aware of the power of attraction to consciously and unconsciously influence and motivate others.

4. Be aware that attractiveness increases your chances of being a target. Accept that some people will be drawn to you for your looks alone. Scrutinize them carefully and practice the uncomfortable need to correct behaviors on the spot.

5. Beauty: don't dismiss it, don't ignore it, and don't abuse it through arrogance and unprofessional behavior. Manage it for the resource it is.

6. Make it a priority to have a confidante to share closed-door or water-cooler conversations about any conscious or unconscious behavior that is hindering your professional growth and that is important to how you want to be/or not be perceived.

9
TRUST BUT VERIFY

"Love all, trust a few, do wrong to none."— *William Shakespeare*

Ana is a twenty-four-year-old personnel manager from Las Vegas. She is a stylish blonde with an artistic style who projects confidence and sense of individuality. She sought out coaching to help her manage her struggle with projecting personal beliefs and values into her relationship with her boss. This story underscores the importance of finding professional balance between personal beliefs and organizational culture and values.

Ana learned one of her most important lessons about trust from a former boss. At that time she was working for a successful real estate investor and restaurateur whose hard and realistic views would eventually change her perception and thoughts on everything.

This was our third call-in session and one sequence of powerful questions to help her think through her personal beliefs triggered a moment of self-realization when she began to tell the story of when she first decided to confront her boss.

ANA

"I was taught to always trust people, to give them the benefit of the doubt up front," Ana confessed. "I always did that even in situations when I knew it wasn't the smart thing to do."

I worked in a family-owned retail store for about two years as a marketing representative until I was appointed to personnel manager, which included responsibilities of making midday bank deposits. After the fifth deposit, the bank teller would comment that there was an extra five dollars in the total count that wasn't recorded on the ledger. Each time, she would ask if I wanted to include it or keep it. This continued each day for nearly two weeks, different teller, same over count, same amount.

I didn't quite understand it but each time, I would return it to my boss and mention rather redundantly that he had over counted by $5.00. Frustrated and somewhat annoyed, I finally decided to confront him.

Mr. Davies was in his office as usual, sitting behind a large oak desk and watching cameras that were placed throughout the store. His money counter was on the table with bills lying next to it. I was sure the five dollar overage had already been accounted for and inserted into the deposit drop.

Frustrated by now, I asked the question that had been bothering me for so long.

"Why don't you just trust that I'm going to make the deposit and if I find any discrepancies, I will bring it to your attention?"

I spoke hesitantly but clearly. I argued that after two years, I earned the position which should have entitled me to a reasonable amount of trust. I had proven myself to be punctual, dependable and committed to the team. Customers and staff gave me high marks because I was always there for them. I took on extra work and they could count on me to be there. These were the values I learned at home, along with the importance of trusting others. I told him that was what I expected and it should be returned. It also didn't hurt to mention that despite being approached by other agencies, I chose to stay, not because I was making more money, I was not. It was because I was loyal and that I knew it was hard to find in an employee in the marketing and sales business.

When I finished, Mr. Davies peered over his glasses. He had the look of someone who was not in the least interested or even moved by my passionate plea. He looked back down at the pad in his hand and then at the cameras that showed every room in the building with the exception of the bathrooms. He was wearing another $1,000 suit and sitting in a large oversized leather chair. His cufflinks looked expensive. I imagined they were not a gift, but an investment in himself.

"You don't give trust. Trust is something that is earned," he said.

He never glanced away from the camera. He spoke firmly and emphatically as if I should know better.

I stood there stunned. His words washed over me like ice cold water and they went against everything I knew. It was a choice that I had not been presented with before.

At this point, Ana paused in her recollection and seemed to go back to that time. As I watched her I understood that what her boss was actually doing was being nonjudgmental. So, it made sense. Ana didn't want to judge people either. In retrospect, she had to ask herself how many times she had given trust only to be taken advantage of. The unfortunate thing was that she would give trust over and over again. The only requirement abusing that trust was a sincere apology. She eventually learned to move away from these people but she'd always meet more. At this point, Ana admitted that she was out at least $3,000 in still unpaid loans to friends, exes, and coworkers.

Ana was one of those women who seemed to have something going on, but, you never knew what that was, exactly. Maybe it was the hair thing. She had a short, sassy boyish cut that framed her round, pixie face. Her makeup was soft and everything about her glowed. Her green eyes were framed by thick eyelashes with no need for mascara. Her fuchsia colored lips were full and dimples appeared on each cheek as she spoke. Ana was a daddy's girl. Though she had no children she quietly wished for a family. While friends were getting married, she worked and traveled. Now recovering from a recent work-love triangle, she was still figuring things out.

She wasn't sure why she always gave trust so prematurely or how it became a sort of peace offering that signaled the commencement of a new relationship of any kind. She had witnessed results of blind trust that lead to pain and the destruction of numerous lives of strangers and friends alike.

She knew the warnings her mother had given her. "People have been killed by other people's good intentions." She would say following the report of some tragic event. Surely, that message continued to be reinforced by everything and everyone around her. Even people who were the least trustworthy seemed to act as if they deserved another chance. Wasn't this expected of us, to be non-judgmental and forgiving?, Ana wondered.

Not according to Mr. Davies.

I worked for Mr. Davies for another year and watched as he applied this principle to everyone he met. I adopted his view of trust in my life and looked at everything differently—my friends, my past, my family and my future. It reordered my thinking, which shifted slowly and with difficulty. Like a cargo ship weighted down but forced to turn at sea.

Now, years later, I continue to observe people I meet, to see where the balance rests. The question provokes more debate than answers. The most intriguing response to this question of giving or not giving trust came from a friend in the military. Tyrone was a young veteran of the Operation Enduring Freedom and the U.S. led invasion of Iraq.

"Trust, but verify," he told me.

Tyrone was a high school classmate and enduring friend. He was one of those students who was great in sports but lacked the attention span for studying successfully. His military career was spelled out long before he knew it. At 6' 3" tall with a lean muscular build, he was a fitness maniac whose obsession only grew as he got older and more competitive. He loved to excel in physical feats. The military was perfect for him.

"Why do you say that?" I asked.

He explained that it was a matter of security and an added layer of protection in a military environment that was always changing and information continuously evolving.

"It's a matter of protection," he said. "You have to come in with doubt. That way you're never blindsided and you've done your due diligence."

I understood then that for Mr. Davies, it was not personal. In his own way, he trusted me to make the deposits, but he also needed the assurance that he could also trust me to report any discrepancies. Every situation is new and different. Just as Tyrone couldn't blindly trust without verifying, neither I nor Mr. Davies, or anyone else should expect a person to not make mistakes whether intentionally or not. Your life and your time have only one advocate and that is you.

"So, do you trust your friends?" I asked.

"I trust, but I verify." He repeated, while offering that all too familiar smile used to charm his way into many hearts. I got the point.

This was a significant lesson that I wish I had learned ten years ago. I started thinking of all the little things that would have made a difference in my life. There was roommate drama, relationship drama, noticing things missing, and broken promises. In the end, it all added up to me getting stuck paying all the rent and utilities.

Why would I take someone's word that they'll pay me back or respect my feelings when I have absolutely no history of their ability to do so? Giving someone the benefit of the doubt is an overused cliché that probably originated from a debt owed that never materialized.

As for Mr. Davies, I eventually earned his conditional trust, which meant it was temporary until conditions changed, but there is another point to be made. His version of trust was not based on blind trust. It was a situational trust. He trusted me to make the bank deposits and report any overages or miscounts. He still did not trust me with anything else. I had to accept that. After all it was not about me, it was about him and the survival of his business.

What is Your Choice?

Smart women know that trust is a virtue and a trait that is worth giving. Intelligent women understand that trust is unique to each person and the situation; therefore, it is renewable, revocable and contingent. (#DIVAtrustbutverify)

Trust isn't all or nothing. It is not blind. Like all things, trust like any other trait should be cautiously given and managed close to the vest. Trust is not something you blindly give. Break away from early teachings and self-deprecating habits that demand up-front abandonment of your better judgment, safety and tried and true knowledge. Your vulnerability is not to be exposed or taken for granted in the name of relationships, work, career, humanity, or charity.

Five Tips for Managing Trust

1. Trust is a desirable leadership trait.
2. Trust yourself first. If you do not trust yourself, ask why and manage those expectations and the expectations of others.
3. Trust has different meanings to different people. Do not expect that your view of trust is the same as someone else's.
4. Do not assume trust is timeless and transferable. Working with the same person does not translate into trust that is creditable toward new situations.
5. When trust is lost, keep what remains and learn from it.

10
CREATE MULTIPLE VERSIONS OF YOURSELF

"The true sign of intelligence is not knowledge, but imagination... The measure of intelligence is the ability to change." — Albert Einstein

This is the story of Maria Tooprakai Wazir, a twenty-six-year-old Pakistani woman and professional squash player. With the support of her father, Maria lived her childhood masquerading as a boy so that she could participate in sports. Her story is taken from news headlines and illustrates the power and capacity to brand and rebrand yourself to overcome personal and social challenges to realize your full potential.

Imagine reporting to work in a place where everyone was against you, but you had to adapt. The reason they are against you is because of something about you, that, on the face of it, you can't change. It could be your gender, nationality, ethnicity, complexion, height, or physical build. Or it could be environmental, a toxic job, or the misery of not living out your life's calling, such as a writer working as a bookkeeper. People, situations, and cultures extract what they need and throw the rest away.

What would you do if your life depended on you, and only you to make a change?

This ability to change depends on social intelligence, which is one of the most valuable, and also difficult skills to master. It requires engaging in face-to-face interaction with ease and comfort with people across different cultural, national, ethnic, and religious backgrounds and experiences. It requires more than eating at your favorite German or Korean restaurant. It also requires going beyond networking within professional organizations, joining a nonprofit board, collegiate fraternal organizations, and organized public events. These are important business and career-building events, but your social intelligence brand requires a more intimate approach to getting to know people as human beings and individuals. This requires the successful creation of multiple simultaneous relationships with people whom you may have nothing in common.

I couldn't imagine being able to do this successfully until I read Maria's story, who because of her love for sports, disguised herself as a boy to live the life she wanted.

Transforming back and forth between gender and cultures is exactly what Maria did so she could live a more fulfilling life. As a young girl growing up in Pakistan, she noticed the vast difference in how boys and girls were treated. She wanted to excel in sports, but knew her gender and the religious rules that governed women and girls, prevented her from doing this. With the full support and help of her father, she created a new version of herself. She decided to adopt the appearances of a boy when in public.[xx] She transformed and created a different version of herself as a professional Pakistani squash player.[xxi]

Reflecting on her experience living as a boy, Toorpakai says, "I lived two lives as one person...I'm more connected to myself and how I should be."

In her novel, *A Different Kind of Daughter*, Toorpakai tells her story of living as a girl in Pakistan and the realization that by transforming herself into a boy for sixteen years, more opportunities would open up for her.

As a result of her experience, she says, "I'm more connected to myself, who I am, who I should be, and how the society should be."[xxii]

Toorpakai's experience touches on another aspect of self transformation, which involves protecting ourselves from harm. After fleeing the strict culture where she describes women and girls as having so much wasted talent and strength, she felt empowered with two voices.

"They can't see the world, they can't see the beauty outside," Toorpakai said.

Her story tells us that we are not monolithic creatures. We are designed to adapt to our environments and be universal and transformative in all aspects, knowing that this is what works for me in this place at this time in my life.

A valuable message a friend would always say to me was, "some people just don't know when to deviate from the video." He'd say this whenever he was frustrated with customer service and even his own employees. He was referring to training videos that were so common in the industry where he worked. After he transitioned into the military, he would say the same thing about military training videos and just about every canned training message companies prided themselves on providing for the ongoing development of their employees. Today, he still stands by that mantra. It has served him well.

The beauty of life is that it's not a video. You are actively engaged in the moment and each screen will be a different collage of emotions, feeling and experiencing that create our own reality and our own perspective to help us make sense of it.

No two people share the same reality. Begin to immerse yourself in these environments and then transition back and forth as needed until you can be who you really are.

"Intelligence is really a kind of taste: a taste in ideas."
— *Susan Sontag*[xxiii]

People do business with people they like. I've heard this often as a business owner. As a nonprofit employee, the sentiment was the same when my boss would refer to fundraising as "friend making."

Creating multiple versions of yourself in some ways speaks to your personal and social brand. Who is involved with creating your social brand? Ideally it should be you. Your social brand is what you put forth after you create a persona, a public face, from which to project your image. Like celebrities from all genres, politicians, academic scholars, and world leaders, you must create something authentic about yourself that adds recognition and familiarity to people who come to know you.

My father always wore a hat, but he didn't wear just any hat. He wore a fedora style felt hat of deep colors like brown or sage green. It gave him a sense of pride and style and the respect that was expected of a gentleman and likewise returned. Wherever he went, he wore this gentleman's hat. In military fashion, he took it off when inside and before exiting a building, he would get up, reach for his hat, put his finger in the crease, and place it on his head. He looked handsome. But what I realized was that everyone knew my father for his hats. I never saw my father wearing a baseball cap and I'm sure he never did. It was his gentlemanly way of showing respect to himself and others. He was his own brand ambassador.

I have relocated and uprooted my life many times. This displacement did not hinder my involvement with things I cared about. In fact, I used it to open new doors. The first thing I did when entering a new city is to look up my local United Way and request a list of board vacancies. The second action was to call the community foundation if my company was involved with charity work or had a corporate social responsibility (CSR) program. If they did, I'd use it to open doors, introduce myself and ask how you can help. If it was not the time to get involved, I'd ask to be placed on their email distribution list. For you, be sure to add new contacts to your LinkedIn connections. If you're a business owner, join the downtown business association. The group is more intimate and has deeper connections to the community.

I am encouraging you to travel often and start when you're young. Begin by listing the places you'd like to visit. If you have a membership in a professional organization, club, or charity, you may already have opportunities to attend meetings and conferences held throughout the world. If international or distance travel is not an option for you, there are national events held annually that celebrate different cultures.

Form relationships with people in different countries, reach out to them on Skype, see their faces and hear their voices. Your perspective and social range is forever transformed. Your level of knowledge and awareness will grow. Your social and emotional intelligence will be stimulated. Take hold of your social brand and manage it as well as you can. If you don't others may be inclined to do it for you.

What is Your Choice?

To be smart is to know that you are capable of creating profound change for yourself and others. To be intelligent is to understand that you are the energy in the room. As energy, you have the power to be transformative and bring about the things you want to become regardless of the odds. (#DIVAmultiplemes)

To thrive and survive in life requires ongoing scrutiny of relationships and an environmental awareness. These require the critical skills of adaptability and quick thinking to create and sustain relationships. You are not a simple or monolithic creature; you are complex and one who has full command of the gift of self-transforming and shape shifting behaviors. The mastery of our 4D Life Skills gives us the confidence to make ongoing adjustments to our life. It requires a mindset of ongoing transformation and a shifting perspective to our views and attitudes about resiliency and change.

Five Tips for Leading Change in Your Life

1. Find your champion.
2. Immerse yourself in who you want to be. Get to know yourself intimately through learning, self-assessments, and self-discovery through mindfulness, meditation and visualization. Include tangible experiences, which add real meaning to your goals and purpose in life.
3. Acquire leadership skills and practice them daily.
4. Adopt a symbol that can be a bridge or link to your true self. Keep it close and look to it when you are in doubt or uncertain about your next decision. For me this symbol has been the image of a butterfly. It connects me to my past and future. It reminds me of growing up on a ten acre farm that was surrounded by animals and wildlife. We even had an alligator or two living in the neighboring swamp. For me, the butterfly represented transformation, beauty, and interconnectedness with the chain of life. They came in so many colors and flew just high enough to always be within reach. When I wanted peace and quiet, I went outside any watched the butterflies. When I completed my

doctoral studies, my good friend and her mom, my second mom, gave me a crystal butterfly. It meant so much to me and most importantly reminded me that our goals may be high, they may change or transform, but they are always within reach. Today, when I need to clear my mind and listen to my heart, I go outside and look for the butterflies. When I feel stress, doubt, or anxiety, or otherwise need to stop and refocus, I look at the butterfly paperweight that sits on my desk.

5. Look to the goal, focus on the outcomes and the benefits you will bring to yourself and others.

Relationships

Noun: the way in which two or more concepts, objects, or people are connected, or the state of being connected.

Synonyms: connection, relation, association, link, correlation, correspondence, parallel, alliance, bond, interrelation, interconnection.

Others perception of us dictate our ability to motivate and influence. Our relationships consist of our connections, associations, affinity, and interactions with others as individuals or in groups. Strong relationships can have a positive or negative influence in our lives and may surprisingly turn in a new direction as relationships mature. Take care to manage relationships well.

11
PRACTICE SELF-PRESERVATION DAILY

"There is nothing more tragic than to find an individual bogged down in the length of life, devoid of breath." — Martin Luther King, Jr.

Terry is a thirty-two-year-old engineer from Charlotte who felt out of balance with self- identity and connectedness with others. She was about five feet tall, and a quiet and unassuming person who blended into the crowd. She contacted me for coaching to help restore a sense of balance to her life. She anchors these emotions in a story she tells of her college friend, Vanessa, who first inspired her to appreciate her vulnerabilities and design a plan to be mindful of her environment. This story is important because it presents a case of how environments can be deceiving and to use our power to think and make choices that allow us to thrive and survive in life.

TERRY

"We're all being watched you know." Terry said as soon as she sat down in my office. She then took a deep breath and told me about why my longtime college friend Vanessa believed this.

Vanessa was one of those college friends who had a conspiracy theory about everything. She was an engineering major and an Air Force brat who arrived on campus with her own car and a new wardrobe. She was 5' 9" and very thin with long, thick black hair styled into an asymmetric cut that spoke to her bold and brash personality. She was of African-American descent and the pride and joy of her close-knit family. She was destined to be successful.

I appreciated her confidence and certainty compared to my timidity toward people and insecurity about life in general. In college I had no car, a parent who was barely working, and a Wal-Mart wardrobe. Where I would watch the student marches in civil disobedience and protests from afar; Vanessa would create a sign and join in. I admired her for that. She had been empowered to have a voice and to exercise her right and her power to challenge societal norms. Somehow, this bold and brave young woman had taken an interest in me.

I had just left class and I was sitting on the "wall" a popular student gathering area near the center of campus. I had an hour before my next class and decided to review my notes.

"Hi, are you waiting for the next class?" I heard a warm soothing voice and looked up into a pair of curious brown eyes and the beginning of a smile. She wore a v-neck T-shirt and a pair of jeans. Her hair was in a ponytail with the area around her ear shaved into a bald crescent. There were different cuts and shapes going on. I wondered where was the missing flash of blonde, pink or blue hair color to round out her representation of all the latest hair trends.

"Yes, I'm just rewriting some notes so that I can understand them later."

Vanessa and I exchanged names then she sat down and began to tell her story. I listened and wondered why she was talking to me. I was a recluse, painfully meek and shy. It was painfully obvious that I was a gullible small town girl trying to find her voice on a cosmopolitan campus whose diverse student body represented domestic and international students of all races, nationalities, and backgrounds.

As the middle child, I often felt invisible at home. I read books and researched topics online that piqued my curiosity. Through reading biographies, histories, mysteries, and by following numerous social causes, I developed a sense of inner determination to be a part of the larger landscape but lacked the external drive, the kind that involved actually protesting or marching, to make it happen.

Maybe Vanessa could see that. She was an advocate for numerous causes and expressed these in mail campaigns or participating in student rallies about everything from war, to torture, social justice, to women's rights in Brazil.

On this particular day when she told me I was being watched, I agreed. In fact, we were all being watched. Advancements in cyber technology, military policing, and street cameras that record every movement was a clear sign that privacy was something of the past.

I assumed she was about to tell me about her latest campaign, but she wasn't.

This was personal. It was about me and who I was as a person. She felt we had to talk.

In the months following our first introduction we became accustomed to each other's personalities and sense of order. According to Vanessa, I liked order, was very judgmental, and carried this sense of silent authority that gave others the impression that I thought I was better than them.

I thought Vanessa was outspoken and outgoing, when compared to my many excursions to the library to surround myself with books. I preferred them much more than people. If someone didn't talk to me, I didn't talk to them. I enjoyed my alone time to think and ponder the future. Vanessa talked to everyone; she invited them to lunch or to events on campus. She "people watched," which she described as some sort of offensive gesture to capture the true spirit of people when they didn't know they were being watched. You can learn so much about people she said, just by observing them.

But there was something not so obvious about Vanessa. Her outgoing, deviant personality and fearless attitude may have, in part, had to do with being the child of a parent who had been raped. Her outgoing and offensive versus defensive personality was just as much of a product of that fact as the decision to fight for social causes. Her mother had taught her that.

Vanessa's mom was our age when it happened. She enlisted in the military immediately after high school and after basic training was assigned to a military installation overseas. This was the first time she would be away from home and she was excited about the opportunity to travel and be a part of something bigger than herself. She was shy and quiet, but she knew if she asserted herself, she could change that and be successful.

A year later, she was very happy and living the life she had dreamed of. She had friends from all over the country. Her supervisor had convinced her to enroll in college and take advantage of the GI-Bill. In four years she could have her bachelor's degree and apply to become an officer. Her pay would then increase tremendously.

"I imagine my mom must have been a very needy person," Vanessa said. "She was looking for affirmation from everyone."

Vanessa's mom, like many young people, had never been taught how to think on their own, at a deeper level. Instead, she expected to be told what to do, what to think and what to say. She became dependent feelings of acceptance and on receiving praise for doing what was expected of her. That gave her validation. It gave her a sense of purpose. The feeling was a calming sedative that guaranteed euphoria from just the right dose. She was the perfect child that any parent would be proud of. Her father's pleased smile and devoted attention was all she needed to get that high.

That neediness eventually led her to misjudge those seeking to offer their help and support. Eventually that led to a night out with friends that ended up in her being led into a dorm room and raped. She thought he was a friend. He was not. He was a predator and he had targeted his victim. He knew her personality, her behavior, and eventually her story. She had confided in him without question because he presented himself as all the things that made her feel safe.

Vanessa's mom never told anyone of the assault even after she became pregnant. Two years later, she was a military mom and college student. She couldn't go back home, she couldn't quit, she decided she would make a life for herself and her daughter. Her rapist in the meantime had moved on to another assignment. They never spoke again.

I reminded Vanessa of the young woman her mother described herself to be. She was right; I was the one who did the homework and gave it out to anyone who asked. I was eager to be nice and supportive to everyone, giving everything and asking for nothing in return.

"My mom taught me to live my life on the offensive," Vanessa said. "I knew karate and boxing, by the age of ten. My mom taught me to be emotionally and mentally flexible in any situation. It's a self-defense mechanism." Vanessa explained, as she pointed her index finger to her temple.

She continued to explain her mental deterrent, which endorsed the use of multiple personalities as some form of psychic defense.

"In some situations I'm a bitch, in others I'm as pleasant as a furry kitten, and in others I stay the background and disappear into the walls. The "bitch" has added years to my life. She can sense trouble in a person's eyes, their tone of voice, and their body language."

Vanessa continued while going from calm to argumentative tones, "These are people who don't respect me and who are looking for me to let my guard down. Instead, I put up a brick wall and dare them to try to put their fist through it. I don't care if I come across as rude. There are young ladies who are missing or hurt today because they didn't want to come across as not being nice. My internal bitch has all of her senses on high alert and she won't let anyone come near me. I know for a fact that she has saved me from harm."

She finished the monologue with a long death stare. Yes, I thought, I can see how that would work. I was definitely afraid.

Taking ownership of your life is a generic cliché. I've only heard it used in the context of career paths, but looking back; I wish someone had explained to me that it meant so much more than that, personally, professionally, and socially. Taking ownership of your life means being on the offensive and dictating how all of your interactions will go.

It simply requires us to be actively engaged in the moment and to push ourselves to develop the assertiveness and confidence to see yourself through to your goals.

Vanessa and I came in and out of each other's lives over the next four years. I always felt she was watching out for me. I graduated the summer before her and then moved to take a job in another state. I regretted not saying goodbye.

> *"It takes something more than intelligence to act intelligently."*
> — *Fyodor Dostoyevsky, Crime and Punishment*

Who We Are Now Determines Our Future Selves

Vanessa and I ran into each other in North Carolina. We were both working in the same city. It was refreshing to see her again. We had matured. She was working at the Environmental Protection Agency, the EPA, and I was celebrating my tenth anniversary at my job. Neither of us was surprised at our chosen occupations. I hid myself in research and writing, while Vanessa was advocating for solar energy and climate change initiatives. Her hair was now naturally black and full of spiral curls that framed her face and shoulders. As we sat on a park bench we began to reminisce. Vanessa had been very influential in my life as a friend and a personal advocate. She taught me how to be noticed as a person and not as a victim or target. I attended my first women's rights rally back then and began taking electives on self defense. My favorite was and still is kick boxing.

"Do you remember that button you used to wear?" Vanessa asked. I honestly couldn't, there may have been many.

"It read Self Preservation."

"Oh my gosh; I can't believe you remember that." I had a moment of surprise and self-respect for the gutsiness of such an act. "Oh yes, I remember!"

It was during the time of my transformation when I was becoming more assertive and more selective in my giving of time and talent. I was walking by the normal gathering of campus vendors and came across a small black button, no larger than an inch in size with the phrase *Self Preservation* in red italicized letters. It moved me. That pin was my first personal demonstration, or rather public outcry, and statement about myself.

My newfound perspective did not come with a sudden burst of all knowing, fearless pursuit of world order, at least in my world. This silent, one woman demonstration was something I had not planned.

The message was clear; self-preservation was what I needed in my life. It was time to focus on myself and to make myself a priority and not to prioritize others.

I adopted that slogan as the mantra for my own personal struggle. It was a protest against everyone who had taken advantage of me, treated me badly, or thought I was a pushover. It was also a protest against anyone who thought I so needed to be acknowledged that I would jump through hoops to make them happy.

What made me decide to take it on as my personal statement? It was a profound set of behaviors and resulting experiences that I predicted would result in my own harm if not attended to. Those experiences centered on discovery of sexuality, religion, self-awareness, and intuitiveness that brought about an ability to predict or foreshadow what my behaviors may create for my future.

It was liberating.

Vanessa had remembered it; I had forgotten. It clearly meant something to her.

At that moment I realized that event as our relationships with friends mature and transform, there is a natural flow from meaningful in the moment to transcending throughout time. They are the validation for your peculiarities, character flaws, and self-assigned soul searching that you have yet to see or acknowledge. They also remember, and can remind you of how far you've come or how far you've deviated from your path.

I wore that pin for the entire semester and I recall that only one person acknowledged it. It was a freshman classmate whom I considered to be a friend. His name was Marcus.

"What does that mean?" Marcus asked, one day during lunch break.

"It means that if I give people the opportunity to take advantage of me, they will, and I have to protect myself." Perhaps he reported back to our classmates because no one asked again.

So on this particular date, nearly a decade of college behind me, Vanessa saw fit to bring it to my attention. It took some time for me to understand how significant this was to her, when I had totally forgotten about it. It also took some time to reflect on how bold it was for me to wear the pin in the first place. Then it hit me that after all those years, I was firmly cemented into her memory and I'd made an impression. I felt proud. That is how we all need to think about our lives.

Leave a Lasting Impression

Looking back now, Terry compared the meaning behind that pin to what I often hear when I'm sitting on an airplane and the stewardess is giving instructions on how to put on the face mask. You first help yourself and then you help others. Like Vanessa, she practices self-preservation by protecting her self-worth so that she is in a strong mental and physical position to be on the offensive and extend a hand to others when she can.

Terry is somewhat embarrassed to say that she has developed three personalities similar to Vanessa's form of offensive and defensive personalities. They are "China Doll," "Foxy Brown," and "Vivian the English Teacher." Each has a social, professional and private role. Her professional persona is Vivian and the one she's least happy with.

"She's too safe and polite," Terry says. "But I need her to deal with managing my professional relationships on the job and my personal relationships at home."

She controls my lifestyle and is always thinking of how to improve it. She makes the biggest contribution to my life and I need her. I just wish she would just step out on a limb and push her hidden talent as a painter and artist a bit further, but she's too practical and too much of a realist. China Doll and Foxy Brown represent my armor for self defense, creative expression and sexual balance. Foxy Brown was inspired by Pam Grier, and was the character she played in her girl-power movies.

Our latent personalities are our gatekeepers as well as our inspiration. They free us up to fulfill the voids in our life and give us the courage to step up to the plate when we need the motivation to do what is necessary to be successful. Self-awareness and self-motivation are the keys to keep moving forward and to be resilient.

What is Your Choice?

To be smart is to know that you must be vigilant in defending and protecting your authentic self on all fronts in life: career, relationships and personal space. To be intelligent is to understand that you are always on alert. Adapt to the environment in which you live, work and play. Be universal and transformative in all aspects. That is what allows you to thrive and survive in this place, at this time in your life. (#DIVAselfpreservation)

Guard the window to your soul. Take care to intimately know your character vulnerabilities and weaknesses so that you can protect yourself from negative or harmful influences. Become skilled at transforming them on command using instruments and assessments to self identify potential character flaws and the skills to nurture and develop them into strengths.

Seven Tips for Safety and Security

1. Take a self-defense course. Make it part of your regular routine.
2. In any and all public surroundings get out of your head and off the phone. Observe people and things.
3. Have a safety plan and a safety routine.
4. Make it a point to learn as much about people as you learn about yourself.
5. Be aware of your vulnerabilities and weaknesses. They may look like opportunities to others.
6. Keep an open and alert mind. Assume nothing.
7. Don't give blind trust, ever.

12
KNOW YOUR PRICE AND WORTH

"Confidence is a sweet spot between arrogance and despair." — Rosabeth Moss Kanter

Trina is a twenty-nine-year-old broadcaster from Oklahoma City who contacted me for professional development and an assessment of her worthiness and readiness to change careers. Her story is anchored in perceptions that challenge her ability to see her own self-worth and professional value. This message is important because it illustrates the importance of letting go of irrational beliefs and fallacies.

TRINA

I've learned a lot from movies. And one of those great lessons was a piece of advice a mother gave her daughter in the movie *The Joy Luck Club*. I can't remember the exact scene, but the phrase I do remember is, "You don't know your worth." It was said during a moment when her daughter was showing signs of helplessness and failure. After all, she had married into wealth, had a beautiful home and a faithful husband who loved her. He had stood up to his parents when they questioned her Asian heritage. She had given up her career to be a stay-at-home mom and was raising a beautiful daughter. But, four years into the marriage, they had fallen into a routine of normalcy. Now they were discussing divorce. Neither could explain what happened to their marriage. What could be wrong?

For me, that scene and her mother's words finally answered a question that had gone unanswered since college. It gave me permission to continue in the direction I was going despite my sense of uncertainty and fear about the unknown. For the full story, I have to go back to my freshman year of college and my first pair of roommates, Lourdes and Rebecca.

It was rush week and Lourdes, Rebecca, and I had been crammed into our 12x15 foot freshman dorm room while waiting on housing to sort out the overcrowding mix up. Upperclassmen were already walking the halls looking to get first dibs on what they called "fresh meat." With rush week in full swing and frat parties each night before courses officially started, it was more of a coed open house than college. It was the first weekend on campus and we were eagerly dressing for sorority and fraternity parties and discussing our curiosities about each other.

"I want to be a nurse." Lourdes said, with the confidence her parents had instilled in her. I imagined she was a symptom of spouse regret, the child of a parent who chose the wrong spouse and lived each day determined to pre-select a prized son-in-law or daughter-in-law.

Lourdes continued to speak as though anticipating the next question.

"My aunt is a nurse," she stated. "I always wanted to be one until I was about nine, that's when I decided I wanted to be a writer."

"Oh," I said with a curious frown.

Lourdes turned each cheek to apply a generous amount of pink blush and glanced over at my expression as if she'd sensed my reaction. I waited for more explanation.

"I want to marry a doctor so I need to be nurse. But writing is my true passion."

Ever since she was old enough to comprehend English, Lourdes's mother told her she would marry a physician. "'Not one of those every day doctors' she would say, like a chiropractor or scientist, but a genius like a heart or brain surgeon." She confided that her mother named her Lourdes because it sounded more appealing for a physician's wife than a Joyce or Alice. Just think of it, all royalty titles end in 'es'; Princess, Duchess and Countess.

She left off mistress, I thought as I tried to apply cheap mascara to uncooperative eye lashes. Lourdes continued. "In my mom's opinion, physicians are respectable, hold the highest position in the community, and make a great income, so we would always be well off.

Lourdes was a beautiful girl, really, I mean stunning. She was model material, but her slender 5' 5" frame probably didn't fit into the type who would retire at the old age of twenty-one and run off with a rock star like Mick Jagger. However, that didn't matter; her full blonde tresses were a beautiful even after years of color treatments. She had naturally full lips and a sculpted nose that would get her far with the pre-meds. I wondered how much surgery she'd already had.

Vanity was an expensive thing, and I imagined that for her mother, it was going to payoff, even if it broke her.

That aside, Lourdes was the complete package. Hard work and good grades at an elite private high school were stepping stones to two things: One being in a good university with a top-ten medical school and two: was a nursing program she could be admitted to. As president of her high school nurses club and a strong list of volunteer activities at local hospitals, she had excellent references and a well-rounded background that secured her fate as a new student at Baltimore's elite university and medical program. Lourdes had been given a mindset for success that gave her little room for deviation. She believed herself to be a commodity from early on.

As we navigated the corners of the narrow room from hair to makeup and then clothes, Rebecca returned from the community shower down the hall. A bunk bed and a rollout left little space for the desk shoved against the wall and closets already full of Lourdes's clothes. Unfortunately, I had been the last to arrive and took the leftover cot and the inch of space left in the closet. My trunk of remaining clothes served as both the coffee table and a dining table for two.

Rebecca quickly moved over to the bed and replaced the towel previously wrapped around her body with a pair of shorts and a tank. We moved over to our next station. I removed my curlers and stood in front of the mirror hanging on the door. This was the hair station. Lourdes finished her makeup at the desk, sat on the coffee table and began applying lotion to her, salon-tanned skin. She left the array of beauty and hair products on the desk for Rebecca's use.

I was the odd one in the cramped room. It never occurred to me to double up on a future aspiration such as career and marriage. Until a few moments ago, I thought they were two separate things. Even Rebecca seemed to have the same perception of the purpose of a college education. You prepared for an education and you came out ready for marriage and homemaking. Preplanning of this magnitude seemed to have been the ritual of their young lives. I envisioned a hospital birthing room filled with a young mother's fairy tale ambitions and the legacy of her mother's ambitious (Lourdes's grandmother) to guide them.

My story was different. I was the second in my immediate family to attend college. My mother and anyone else who spoke to me about school expected me to make good grades so that I could get an education. Two of my aunts and an uncle had bachelor's and master's degrees and were successful by my family's measure, which meant they drove expensive new cars. My mother on the other hand had been passed over. That dream was given to her sister instead of her.

"I got married very young and was pregnant with you when I was nineteen." My mother had confided in me. She was working in retail at the time and just wanted to save enough to buy a car. When she became pregnant, she took some online courses but did not finish. My dad worked at the lumber mill and did his best to take care of us.

My great grandmother primarily cared for me while my mom and dad worked. She expected me to be independent and that meant to finish college and to get a good job. Her dream for me wasn't to find a husband or go to college; it was to have a career and the ability to support myself no matter which route I took. She and the rest of the women in our family reared their children, as a team. They understood that dreams are fleeting like marriages. They wanted security for their daughters; a male provider was secondary.

For me, at that time in my life, a husband was on a distant shoreline, not an anchor to build my life around.

The different approaches to weighing what was valuable to Lourdes and Rebecca always bewildered me. For the most part, it was indicative of the amount of planning and focus that dictated our lives from an early age. What engendered it or from where the first thought originated baffled me. I had my suspicions, but I carried this annoying question about the outcome. Did it really work?

The answer finally occurred to me while watching the movie, *The Joy Luck Club*. I could finally explain that nagging feeling about the choices these women made. "You don't know your worth." This sentence spoke volumes.

The fact is, women do know their worth. This is associated to the level of confidence in their ability to create the vision they want for themselves regardless of the status of their current relationships. More importantly, she is the only person who is capable of self-appraisal that requires personal reflection of her individual contributions and a healthy perspective of the value and meaning of the outcomes of her work across her LifeSpace.

I suppose the dilemma for me was that the question of falling in love was not the issue. I could see that happening for Lourdes and Rebecca. Some of us fall in love many times over and some of us do not. But if the chance for love does come our way, how can we dictate the occupation, gender, or lifestyle. I couldn't figure that out until then, when it became clear to me that you can't dictate it. At some point you begin to negotiate your personal worth and worse yet, the value of your happiness.

In the movie, it wasn't that they were not in love, it was the way they had drilled down their perfect lives into such a fine-tuned and well-proportioned process that it became mechanical, belittling and petty. The deal breaker was when her husband took out a calculator to determine how to split the grocery bill and reminded her that when they got married, they agreed to split everything fairly. He wasn't taking into consideration the value she brought to the family by raising their child.

Undoubtedly, women must know their worth. We are solely responsible for our lives. When we are alone with no one around us, we must appraise ourselves. These values determine how we approach our relationships in each aspect of our involvement and time spent becomes even more valuable.

Understanding the Difference Between Self-Esteem and Self-Worth

Knowing your worth is a leadership balance between knowing who you are in the workplace as well as who you are at home. The value stays the same even when the environment changes.

Traditionally, value in the corporate world is proven through what contributions you make to the company and in return, they compensate you for what this value is worth to them.

I want to make a critical distinction here because I often sense a confusion among parents and children about the difference between professional value and self-worth as it relates to the workplace. In my experience, the big difference, is professional value is part of the knowledge, skills, and abilities you bring to the workplace. In contrast, self-worth is a personal measure of how you feel about yourself. Generally, I associate it with the level of happiness you feel about your life and the health of your LifeSpace.

Self-worth has much to do with self-esteem. I hear this often coming from parents, teachers, and young people from disadvantaged neighborhoods in the U.S. My though is, unfortunately, so you have self-esteem, now what? Self-esteem is not a career path.

My experience has shown me that so much effort has been spent on building self-esteem that our youth are under the impression that it is all you need to be successful. However, I've never heard the statement, "We hired him or her because they had great self-esteem."

Companies do; however, hire based on character. "Hire character. Train skill" was a statement made more than two decades ago by the chief executive officer of Porsche and it still holds true.

Some have placed all of the value of our net worth, education, training, family, and career squarely on the pretext of a perfect partner or companion. And it was not until we have achieved this goal that we begin to assess our value in whatever context we find a relevant measure.

With these thoughts in mind, unconscious bias sometimes influences our value based on companionship *first*. Success is viewed as a secondary objective or path to achieving the first. The result feeds into the mindset that our contributions to the workplace, or interest in a career, are not a priority as it should be.

Unfortunately, if I were to look at my brother, he was groomed to focus on career first. I on the other hand was groomed to focus on being a lady first. There's a big psychological disadvantage and research shows that women's inability to ask for equal pay for equal work reflects this disadvantage. It's a matter of confidence says the American Association of University Women (AAUW) who has initiated the conversation on gender and equity in pay.[xxiv]

What is Your Choice?

To be smart is to know that you have value and self-worth. To be intelligent is to understand that this is relative to how much power you give away, whether consciously or unconsciously. It is your responsibility to recognize your worth, assess what adds value, and what needs further development for your satisfaction. (#DIVAknowyourprice)

Inventory your skills and talents as a friend, colleague and family member. Go ahead, write them down and create a list. Understand that this list has exponential value to others and create a plan that uses these assets to your benefit. And, also recognize which assets are most likely to be perceived as skills and talents others are more likely to appreciate or exploit.

The advantage of hiring a new employee with confidence and clarity of purpose for their own strengths and weaknesses cannot be undervalued. Employers have a host of employability factors to consider before hiring a potential employee. Self-awareness is an appreciating skill that shapes insight into who we currently are so that we can work toward goals to develop the soft skills that inform more intelligent behaviors. This is a critical factor in hiring and firing, upward mobility, and team building. Self-awareness is critically important in job interviews when soft skills such as sociability, likability, and fit, determine the decision to hire, even if the hard skills may not be fully developed. The difference is that hard skills are easier to develop, soft skills are not.

As a professional coming into a career field, transitioning from a career change, or if you are an entrepreneur seeking contracts, your advantage is in knowing exactly what you have to offer as a self-starter. That knowledge begins well before the interview.

Six Tips to Evaluating Self Worth

1. Self-inventory your skills, talents; strengths and weaknesses.

2. Ask your close friends to list your five assets or strengths and weaknesses. Do the same with colleagues.

3. Look to job evaluations for work assessments and pay attention to the areas you want to develop.

4. Stay abreast of what industry skills are more valuable and marketable.

5. Character and personality multiply the value of technical skills and talents. Focus on these areas with equal effort. They add the most worth over time.

6. Take action to challenge yourself and stretch your abilities to ensure you are continuously authenticating your talents by using them to create forward momentum in your life.

HOW RELEVANT IS SELF ESTEEM?

"Self-efficacy is the term that psychologists use to describe the belief a person has that says they can reach their goals. Unlike self-esteem which is more of a global judgment on the self and its worth, self-efficacy specifically isolates the way an individual assesses their competence in relation to achievements, goals and life events."

The Center for Confidence and Well-Being, UK, argues that self-esteem refers to how a person feels about themselves. Self-efficacy is about a person's confidence that they can take action toward achieving their goals. In other words, self-esteem refers to feelings about the self overall.

A summary of their research on the factors related to high and low self-esteem is illustrated in the following table. Note, that self-esteem is irrelevant for academic performance, and many job related or performance related activities.

A SUMMARY OF THE EVIDENCE ON SELF-ESTEEM

High self-esteem is positively correlated with:
- initiating relationships with others (moderate correlation)
- sexual experimentation in young people
- racist attitudes
- violence (bullies, sociopaths, etc., report high self-esteem)
- speaking out in large groups
- achieving goals through self-regulation
- happiness
- better management of stress so some positive health outcomes

Low self-esteem is positively correlated with:
- teenage pregnancy (only one of a number of factors)
- eating disorders (again only one of a number of factors)
- teenage smoking in girls (but could lower self-esteem then be the cause?)
- unemployment/low income in males
- vulnerability to depression
- suicide and suicidal thoughts
- victims of bullying

Self-esteem is irrelevant for:
- academic performance
- many job or performance tasks
- alcohol or drug abuse

Source: Creating Confidence Handbook, Center for Confidence and Well-Being

13
ADAPT AND OVERCOME

"With the new day comes new strength and new thoughts." — *Eleanor Roosevelt*

This is my personal narrative, which was inspired by the 2016 U.S. presidential election and advocates for expanding personal boundaries to foster better understanding and empathy with others. Commit to being a champion for the creation of new relationships beyond existing comfort zones. To achieve the outcome you desire, increase your social and emotional intelligence that will give you the confidence to start conversations with people you do not know.

BROOKS

It's now a week after the 2016 U.S. presidential election. Some historians say Nostradamus predicted it.

Like so many, I feel numb and short of breath. I do not feel angry. I feel empty. I don't know if I'm breathing, or if the short gasps of pain are signs of a soul gone hollow. One that has left the body and its remaining energy is rushing around the inside of the empty shell trying to stop the vacuum and fill the void.

I know that I am not who I was on November 7; I wasn't damaged then. I felt connected like part of something complicated and extraordinary with flaws and deep caverns and sunlight and shooting stars all working in tandem to make some sense of order and mystery for me to explore as part of my gift of life.

I was supposed to be a part of something big that would shape the future and bring hope to women and children globally. We would save the earth with an orgasm of democracy—the first full climax of its kind. Humanity had been waiting for it so long, and we were almost there.

I could feel my pulse increasing, my heart pounding. I felt warm and hot and breathless. I envisioned colors of a galaxy nebula with wings shaped like those of a butterfly. We were about to transcend into a new universe where all things and people would be welcome and free—free to live and create. It was a place where we would all be equal.

Then, suddenly, it vanished into thin air just before the euphoria was about to come rushing through my body.

I closed my eyes and sought out silence. For days, I avoided the television and the public. I couldn't bear to hear the voices and see the faces of celebration and sadness. As the sting began to wear off, I wandered into the night to look for my people. I found my tribe gathered in the safe walls and comforting books of an Indie bookstore. I drank wine and ate cheese and crackers until it began to feel like it was a new kind of sober. For a moment, I felt happy, safe and calm. I'm still waiting for the climax that my mind knows will not come, not now, not ever.

Today, I turned on the television for the first time following the election. President Obama was speaking. I needed to hear his voice of calm sobriety and reason. He delivered a message of hope and optimism for a standard of "better." Surely we as a nation could achieve that, together. I knew I would miss him, the same way I would miss Hillary.

I started to think of the lessons and what I was supposed to do next. I felt the oncoming tinge of inspiration; it was the small rhythmic feeling of a pulse, weak but still fighting to get stronger. I would live again. All had not been lost.

Then I thought of her and what she would want me to do. I had changed. Had she changed too, not likely I thought; no, not at all. She was a fighter. She would continue to fight…for "better" too. She would need me again.

How could I begin to get ready to prepare myself and to never turn around to look back? Hadn't she told us to keep moving? That was after her first loss.

I knew there would be distractions.

I searched my soul for that new meaning. The message I was supposed to receive that carried the new lessons that were supposed to help me grow. I imagined that my mind was a computer processing code. What was the input, the output, the meaning?

Don't Question? -----Do it. -----Now. -----Repeat.

Don't Question? -----Do it. -----And again. -----Repeat.

Don't Question? -----Do it. -----Now. -----Repeat.

Don't Question? -----Do it. -----And again. -----Repeat.

What is it that I shouldn't question? Myself.

I have learned that all the excuses of why I can't had been disproven.

You're not experienced, it doesn't matter.

You're a woman, it doesn't matter.

You're black, it doesn't matter.

You're young, it doesn't matter.

You're short, it doesn't matter.

So what matters? If, they like you more.

How can I get them to like me?

I must adapt and overcome any and every obstacle. Adapt and overcome was a statement about resilience. I remembered that message. My mom and dad taught me that.

Times change, people change, situations change, environments change, things change. It's inevitable and it's completely within our control. Adjusting to the moment means taking advantage of the opportunity to reset your pace and change course at any given moment when things are not going as expected. It means that when an environment or situation doesn't feel quite right, get out and readjust your thinking and your behavior. If your current situation isn't working, then it's time to take a bold step to shake loose the hinges and readjust them.

I can do that. I can do that now.

So what is important today?

It is important to set goals and lay out a plan to achieve these goals. This is tantamount to the realization of my awesomeness. It's important to continuously check my ambitions against the reality of the environment. Sometimes, a temporary deviation will come and I will be ready and open to adding important lessons that will improve upon my initial plans. I will be better armed to open doors that I had not even thought about approaching.

It is important for me to find my tribe, my people; to use that energy for good. I will need their energy to keep me strong. I will stick to the end plan while managing the timeline and considering all alternate routes and options to get there.

I'm *still* with Her.

What is Your Choice?

To be smart is to know that situations are temporary and change is ongoing. To be intelligent is to understand that living demands growth that comes through active engagement with all people and ideas. (#DIVAadaptandovercome)

The importance of setting goals and laying out a plan to achieve these goals is tantamount to the realization of our awesomeness. However, this is easier said than done when we are ignorant of our strengths. These are the natural talents we are born with and when we enter a task from a position of strength, rather than weakness, we are more likely to be happy and successful. Strengths Based assessments are instrumental in determining how you need to approach your plans and goals. With strength as your mental armor, begin to take action and continuously check our ambitions against the reality of the situation. Adapt and adjust along the way while changing tasks to fit the moment. Stay focused on the desired outcome, manage the timeline, and consider all alternate routes and options to get there.

Six Tips to Managing Societal and Cultural Change

1. Look to opportunities that are always present.
2. Adopt new skills, refine others.
3. Form new alliances with groups and organizations.
4. Look in the mirror and take responsibility for your choices.

5. Step outside of your boundaries and talk to people you do not know. Seek to understand their stories and their ideas without judgment, bias or the impulse to draw conclusions.
6. Practice empathy.

14
ELIMINATE JUDGMENT

"Be curious, not judgmental." — *Walt Whitman*

Victoria is a thirty-six-year-old part-time teacher and admissions officer from Houston. She is a smart and quick-witted professional who sought coaching to help her let go of limiting beliefs and personal values that were effecting her ability to start and maintain relationships critical to her job. Her coaching experience started with Mrs. Singe, her boss and a proven leader in her profession, who opened the door and became Victoria's mentor and champion. Her story is important because it shows the impact of assigning labels and judgment that distort reality.

VICTORIA

The most difficult life skill that I have had to master was my unhealthy use of judgment and my inability to distinguish it from opinion, assessment and decision making. In the end, I had to address them one by one with the last informing my choice of graduate studies. It bothered me that much because so far, the result of my use of judgment had resulted in embarrassment and avoidance, and it was affecting my ability to improve my performance on the job. It was such a subconscious or act that I didn't even know I was doing it until it was too late. By then, my personal credibility or much worse, my job credibility, had been lost.

Let me start at the beginning and where my confusion with judgment started.

The first place I heard about this thing called judgment was at church. The church my family attended was a small wood frame, single story structure with chipping white paint. It sat on a cement base of brick blocks raised over open ground. The front steps led to two red entry doors that swung open when the choir came marching in. The towering black cross was nailed to the façade and it looked strong and dominant as if it was built to hold up against the strongest storm. I remember standing in front of that white church with the red doors at the age of eight and it looked massive. It would be the fourth place of worship my single mother would take us. I wondered why we had to leave our grandparents church and why we passed so many just to get to that one. Our new church was an hour's drive away.

Only five of the six of us children could fit into the 1980s Buick Regal. Two alternated each week. When my grandmother joined us, three would have to stay home. My siblings and I coveted the day when our turn to stay home was up. We knew we were unfortunate souls about to miss an inspiring and revolutionary message that was sure to come that day.

We did this routine three times a week. Monday was bible study, Wednesday was choir rehearsal and Sunday was the sermon. The gas for the car alone seemed to take up most of our modest means. Then there was the offering, which sometimes came twice a day. One was for the building fund and the other for the general offering.

The sermon repeated itself over the years, which seemed appropriate for the changing faces in the congregation to have the opportunity to hear it. I enjoyed the music of the old church with the multiracial congregation and the nondenominational message. The only thing that changed for certain was the makeup of the fifty-member congregation that sometimes dwindled to as much as twenty.

Reverend Press was in his early seventies. He opened his sermons with news of wrath and love and obedience. Love thy neighbor as thyself and live as the fearful servant of a loving God. The rules were simple it seemed. Follow the Ten Commandments. Practice Chastity. Believe in the Father, The Son, and The Holy Ghost. Those who are without sin shall cast the first stone. These spoken words and their underlying meanings were reinforced at home.

The male elders sat in the pulpit or along the right front pew. They ran the business affairs of the church. Their wives sat in their white dresses. Lace scarves covered their heads when ready to take sacrament. The patriarchal structure was strong and ever present. The reminders of these themes were never-ending. Society mirrored them with more of the same. Anything that didn't fit these models was looked upon with criticism and disapproving eyes. That was where my confusion about judgment began.

My unlearning didn't start until I left home and moved into an apartment that I shared with a classmate. My first embarrassing moment with a stranger came soon thereafter.

"What is going on with that guy with the ponytail and messy beard? He's such a homeless person." I said with big disapproving frown. Carla smiled and dismissed my comment with a look in a direction opposite mine.

My friend and I were at a charity event and proud of our new found charitable ways. I had a passion for the elderly, which was in large part because of my mom's work as a nursing aid at a senior retirement facility. When they held special events such as birthday parties and holiday gatherings, I would go in costume. My best memory was when I dressed as an elf and sang to the residents. It gave them such joy that I insisted on doing it every year until couldn't wear the outfit anymore. After that I would come wearing a birthday hat or T-shirt that proclaimed Happy Birthday. Mom loved caring for the elderly. It was the one place that I remember where she was always happy.

My friend Carla loved working with the local farmers market. Her dream was to bring healthy food to the homeless. Her idol was then First Lady Michelle Obama.

On this occasion, we decided to buy tickets to a fundraising event hosted by the local Rotary Club. There were about 200 people in attendance from many different organizations and businesses. There was no particular dress code for the after-five event, but the majority of people appeared to be business employees. At some time during the event, we noticed an older man with his hair in a long ponytail. He was unshaven and wearing clothes that didn't meet the neat test according to my very important standards.

Based on his appearance, I very quickly surmised that he was homeless. I continued to glance in his direction to see if he was with someone. He was not. I thought about how nice it would be of me to talk to him and offer him help. I noticed that he wasn't talking to anyone and chose to stand alone in the back of the room. I decided to approach him to ask if he was okay or if he needed anything.

"No, I'm fine he replied." I was sure his polite smile mirrored mine.

Determined to show my concern, I asked if he lived at one of the local shelters.

He looked confused, then taken aback.

To my embarrassment, this man not only had a home, he was a retired physician with a beautiful house and a loving family in it. After showing some amusement at my judgment, he then explained that his hair was the result of a lost bet.

"I can't cut it for a year," he said with a warm smile. I have a month to go and I will then cut it and donate it to charity.

He was attending the event to support a charity that worked with cancer patients.

I felt ignorant and small. Carla again expressed her displeasure not with a word but with a smile I knew all too well. The one that said there you go again thinking you know everything.

At that point in my life, I'm sure I had unintentionally burned enough bridges. My immature assumptions and behaviors showed that I was as much of a social liability as I was a skilled and talented employee. My assumptions, based on immature judgments exposed a lack of maturity and experience in communicating and working with people. When working as an individual, I excelled. When working in a team, I was not as effective.

My behavior reminds me of a quote I often say to young people today. "When you judge others, you don't define them, you are defining yourself." It summed me up in twelve words or less.

Judgment is a funny thing because it is evenly exercised by the most intelligent and the most ignorant people. In my home, it was contagious. Everyone at every age and level of experience practiced it. And when it doubt, there was always a statistic, bible verse, or statement of unknown fact to reinforce it. Unfortunately, I took these habits and behaviors into the workplace and applied them to my life experiences without really realizing they were stifling me.

I wasn't fully freed of these damaging thoughts and resulting behaviors until I was nearing thirty when finally, I realized everything that I saw, heard, and experienced was the result of deeply held beliefs that were not grounded in reality.

It didn't happen by trial and error, but because I was fortunate to have a boss who was highly intuitive and aware. Mrs. Singe was our chief operating officer and I was her director of programs. On any given day, no matter what was happening, she seemed to know the pulse of the office. It didn't require anyone saying anything; she was very connected to the energy and emotions of others. She could see right through me.

When I was having a really difficult week, she called me into her office and began to talk. She talked about her kids, her week, her goals and personal frustrations, and she talked about me. It's clear to me now that she was coaching me. In some ways she saved my life and my career. I don't mean in a life or death sort of way, but from a quality of life perspective.

For the first time, a person was teaching me how to think and make decisions. All of my life, I had been told *what* to think. As an adult, it was time to learn *how* to think. It starts with one simple predisposition she said, and that is to understand that I know absolutely nothing. She asked me to envision it and to my surprise it was effortless.

I experienced overwhelming sensation of standing in an open doorway with a strong sweeping breeze surrounding me as it passed through the open halls and towering columns between flowing archways. The breeze didn't settle but continued to enter from one direction as if it was traveling through to an unknown destination, the source was unknown. My mind felt powerful and free of restrictions and constraints. I inhaled all of it, it was clean and fresh. I breathed differently. I felt cleansed. I felt stress free. I felt happy.

Mrs. Singe went on to explain how her career had taken off, she was an orphan abandoned by both parents and lived in foster homes for as long as she could remember. Each household was different and had a different approach to teaching. Eventually, she learned that it wasn't so much about her, but it was all about her conforming to their lifestyle. Most of the families viewed her as something they felt sorry for and needed to save. She never knew what they were saving her from, but regardless, she was viewed as a victim of circumstance and they wanted or needed to shelter her.

They had their motivations as well. In some cases she was a contributing member of the household. She referred to it as free labor. Sometimes there would be multiple foster children contributing to the household. In the beginning, she felt that if she worked hard, she could stay. In any case, assuming what they wanted failed. Judging them was a disaster. Being curious about them worked.

What my boss explained was her discovery that personalities and motivation were the two things she needed to be mindful of about people. In order to get ahead, she had to appreciate everyone's motivations and desires without the need to draw inferences or conclusions. To do so often lead to outcomes she did not want or intend.

Her approach to life was that simple and it gave her a strong appreciation for the unknown. "I learned to focus on emotion and what is felt by paying attention to what is not said, what is not shown," she said.

She transitioned out into a halfway house at eighteen and started working for a hotel chain where she began to excel. Mrs. Singe had a knack for people and for understanding their needs. She quickly moved up the ladder and eventually crossed over into vendor sales and now heads the corporate division. She was firm on policy and customer service, but she was open and negotiable when it came to people.

"We hire for skill, and we do train for emotional intelligence," she said. "Many companies do not."

I had focused my entire life on developing the skills and talent to be competitive in any job or career that I wanted. Today, I was being told that it wasn't enough.

In life, it wasn't what I thought about things or people that were so important. It was about my ability to persuade them. People have opinions on everything. It's how I communicate, engage, and relate to others that determine if they will listen in the first place.

I had to unlearn my fixed mindset and faulty thinking and judging behavior. I had to evolve into a self-aware and emotionally intelligent person who was open to hearing and empathizing with the experiences of others. People will naturally see the value it adds to everything you are a part of.

What I eventually recognized was to be curious about people was a more natural and gracious act. However, that did not extend to a need to answer that curiosity based on my own story. It is up to the person to tell theirs. Everyone has a story. It is their map of the world, their worldview. The odds are that it will be a teachable moment, something that will expand your thinking and leave you more empowered and appreciative than you were before.

What is Your Choice?

To be smart is to know that judgment leads to assumptions and these assumptions close doors and limit progress. To be intelligent is to understand that the mind is open and all experiences and paths to learning are limitless. Judgment is best left to those with limited capacity to understand. (#divaeliminatejudgment)

Judgment, opinion and assumption; these are easily the most destructive words in any language. If it is possible to eliminate any use of it from your thoughts, then do it. Replace it with curiosity and open mindedness that will give you access to a magnificent worldview and space for a new dimension of living and appreciation for learning more about everything.

Nine Tips to Develop Creative Thinking & Curiosity

1. Slow down your thinking enough to hear.
2. Appreciate the value of perspective and look for the context of all things.
3. Do something different that expresses creativity.
4. Listen to the conversations of strangers. You always learn something new and different.
5. Diversify your friendships.
6. Ask more open-ended questions.
7. Travel.
8. Read.
9. Explore your curiosity and take an alternatively safe travel route you normally would not.

SOCIAL & CULTURAL AWARENESS BUCKET LIST

Which of the following statements describe your experience?

1. I have attended an HBCU* sponsored event or visited an HBCU campus.
2. I have had dinner at the home of a family from an ethnic background different from my own.
3. I occasionally listen to urban-based radio programs.
4. I have attended a Native American spiritual or cultural event.
5. I have attended a community event sponsored by a cultural or ethnic group different from my own.
6. I have read a historical or educational book or article about a culture or ethnic group different from my own.
7. I have a close friend, non-coworker, from a different culture or ethnic background who I personally and socially interact with at least once a month.
8. I have attended an HSI* sponsored event or visited an HSI campus.

9. I am a member of a social club or civic association that supports causes benefitting ethnic or cultural groups that are different from my own.
10. I have watched a movie telling the life story of individuals who are not from my own ethnic or cultural group.
11. I am a member of an online community that consists of people from diverse ethnic and cultural backgrounds.
12. I learn about people from different ethnic and cultural backgrounds from personal relationships I have formed.
13. Some of my role models do not look like me or behave like me.
14. I often initiate friendly small talk with strangers.
15. I have attended a Chinese New Year event.
16. I have friends or have established working relationships with people from around the world.
17. I have read popular fiction written by authors of diverse ethnic and cultural backgrounds.

18. I have read the book *From "Superman" to Man* by J.A. Rogers

19. Write in your own bucket list item:

20. Write in your own bucket list item:

Answers: There is no right or wrong answer. The goal is to increase your number of diverse experiences and knowledge.

*The U.S. Department of Education uses the acronym HBCU to refer to Historically Black Colleges and Universities. HSI is the acronym for a Hispanic-Serving Institution.

UNCONSCIOUS AND HIDDEN BIAS QUESTIONNAIRES

Research-based behavior, personality and social assessments are valuable tools to improve self-awareness. There is no right or wrong, just good insight for your own emotional and social development goals.

1. **Teaching Tolerance: Test Yourself for Hidden Bias:**
   http://www.tolerance.org/activity/test-yourself-hidden-bias

2. **Prejudice, Bias and Hate Questionnaire:**
   https://www.monmouth.edu/university/Prejudice_Bias_and_Hate_Survey.aspx

3. **Personal Self-Assessment on Anti-Bias Behavior:**
   http://www.adl.org/assets/pdf/education-outreach/Personal-Self-Assessment-of-Anti-Bias-Behavior.pdf

4. **Barriers and Bias: The Status of Women in Leadership:**
   http://www.aauw.org/research/barriers-and-bias/

5. **Harvard Bias Test – Project Implicit:**
   https://implicit.harvard.edu/

15
GET A REALITY CHECK

"What's terrible is to pretend that second-rate is first-rate. To pretend that you don't need love when you do; or you like your work when you know quite well you're capable of better." — *Doris Lessing*

Elaine is a thirty-one-year-old publicist from Albuquerque who sought help to be more accountable to herself and with addressing uncertainty with life decisions. She uses the analogy of her favorite court television show to illustrate her fascination with hope and her inclination to put that before reality. This story is important because it illustrates how emotional reasoning or all-or-nothing thinking can compromise our most important life decisions and hold us back.

ELAINE

"Fiction is truth in disguise," said Elaine.

While most women were turning to Oprah to add motivation and inspiration to their lives, I was turning to Dr. Laura or Judge Judy for a sense of realism. For me, they were a safe place where feelings can be legally or practically thrown out of the discussion.

I've learned a lot from watching the endless dais of women suing for the return of their dignity and/or the repayment of gifts and loans. It has provided me with enough awareness about my life to last a lifetime.

Elaine expressed feelings of shock at what she felt was the limitless capacity for individuals to take advantage of others and justify it for one reason or another. It didn't matter who they said they were or where they said they came from, they were represented in all sizes, shapes, backgrounds, beliefs, and abilities across the human Diaspora. Some were taken advantage of because of their relationship with what seemed to be a stranger. While others were determined to give to others regardless of any compelling need to do so or in some cases with the knowledge they would likely be victims. Most often it seemed these choices were based on hope or faith or the belief that everyone deserves a chance. Elaine now equated that to a belief in miracles.

The most egregious situation was that of a young disabled woman who was receiving disability assistance and living with her mother. From looking at the young lady you wouldn't be able to tell that anything was wrong with her. She was attractive and was in the beginning of her second career following her disability settlement.

"So what's wrong with you?" The Judge inquired.

"I have a pinched nerve at the base of my spine, Your Honor" she answered.

"You mean you can't stand or sit for extended periods?" The Judge clarified the response she intended to hear.

"Yes, Your Honor."

"Then hurry up!" The Judge exclaimed, already signaling her annoyance. The Judge was known for her raspy accent, which became animated when easily agitated. Clearly, she had been doing this for a long time. Her "you can't fool me" character and intimidation were served even-handedly to all parties and complimented with scolding lips and annoyed eyes.

The case before her was of failure to repay a loan in the amount of $5,000. The woman had loaned her boyfriend the money so that he could make repairs on his fishing boat, which he used for business. The young man's excuse for failure to repay the loan was that it was a gift. Not only was it a gift, he claimed, he never asked for the help. The woman offered him the money because she wanted to help him.

After a few questions and quick exchanges between the parties, the case was over. Without any documentation from the plaintiff that would defend the young woman's claim, the Judge ruled in favor of the defendant.

Television aside, this was happening to Elaine as well. She was one of those people who lived on hope.

What had been challenging for her was to figure out that when a person decides they want something from you, they are going to show you their best self and put on their best appearance. It doesn't have to be an immediate need, but somehow as they assess you and test your capacity to fold against pressure, they eventually come up with a need they feel you may be able to satisfy. Based on our confidence in the relationship, we then put aside any instincts and move forward hoping for the best outcome. The maturity of the relationship didn't seem to matter. What did seem to matter was how important and needed it made the individual who was doing the giving, feel about themselves.

The lesson learned from these examples and her own experiences is that life is sometimes the result of failure to investigate and betting on hope to save the day. Clearly, hope had no value except for chance. It has the same effect as betting on a horse. The best odds are 50/50 if you win or lose, and it goes down from there. Like trust, hope was worthless unless there are signatures on a document. That was the Judge's informed and legal opinion.

BARBARA

A person who was brave enough to tell her story is Barbara. She had been working as an administrative assistant for an insurance company for the past eight years. She was a great employee, always punctual, willing to do her fair share of work, valued her place in the company, and regularly spoke of her activities at the mega church where she was a member.

Barbara was devoutly religious and loved her pastor who delivered his sermons live on multiple networks. She was so devoted that she believed pastors should earn millions and had no problems with their gated estates and private leer jets.

"I think the congregation should purchase a jet for their pastor." She said after the story broke in the news about the pastor's request to his members. He needed a new jet that would allow him to complete his annual missions around the world. It was a part of his ministry she said.

I wondered about the millions of poor and homeless men, women, and children who could receive a hot meal and a roof over their heads with the money a jet would cost.

Over three years, we would talk often during lunch breaks about church and family, but in the years that I worked for the company, I rarely heard her speak about her husband. She was a lovely, high-spirited young woman who had waited for what she described as an eternity to find the right one. Eventually, at the age of forty she met the love of her life. And, he was a man of faith.

"I really had to come to terms with my demons about trusting people." Barbara would say as encouragement to me, the young single girl in the office.

I knew Barbara loved her husband deeply and she openly displayed this affection with pictures of places they had visited pinned all over her small cubicle. I would only meet Barbara's husband once on the occasion when I had to take her home from work. For all the times I had known her, she had never asked for transportation nor had she ever missed a day at work unless she was severely sick or had an illness in her immediate family. I knew this because she would show up for work terribly ill only to be sent back home. She didn't want to let anyone down.

Barbara had been married for four years now and something about her was unraveling, I didn't know what.

The ride to her house was fifteen minutes and her husband was home. Her car was in the driveway and I wondered why he couldn't pick her up.

After about a month and several trips later, she opened up. I guess people at work had started to notice a change in her too.

Barbara was in the middle of a divorce. As the situation unfolded and she began to rely more and more on her small circle of friends at work, Barbara began to reveal a sad and teachable moment for all of us. But for us women, it was particularly illuminating.

Barbara met her husband at a church outing. He was a family member of another parishioner who introduced them. He was a nice local man who worked for a company that managed road signs. He lived with some relatives and had a young son from a previous relationship that ended badly. He worked hard to support his child and to make a life for himself. He relied on the family for their support.

Soon after he and Barbara started dating. He was kind and enjoyed cooking dinners and watching movies on the weekend. He was modest and sincere and very thrifty and Barbara understood that. Eventually they were spending so much time together that family began to ask why he didn't just move into her home. After six months of dating they were very much in love. Following a brief engagement and a lovely small wedding he did just that.

As they began to build a life together, Barbara understood that she had to put all of their belongings in her name because he had terrible credit. They also shared joint checking accounts. In order to free up cash to pay his back child support, she refinanced her home and put it in both their names. She also bought him a dependable car and continued to use her old faithful because of her short drive to work. Barbara wanted to set him and their future straight. She was all in.

A year later, Barbara was struggling. Her credit was now going south and she was overwhelmed trying to pay their expenses. Her husband was working as hard as she was, but all of his income seemed to be going to take care of his son and newly found lifestyle that was taking him away from the church. He was now spending more time hanging out with family and friends. Eventually they were living two separate lives and Barbara was supporting all of it. Against her church and her family's wishes, she filed for a separation, but he didn't leave. Then creditors began calling. She was stressed and unhappy, he on the other hand had nothing to worry about. If he chose, he would walk away in a better position than before. Barbara on the other hand was about to lose everything.

I imagine that for all those years her marriage was going south, Barbara prayed about it and found comfort in her church family. However, I wondered if she would even be in her situation if she would have simply investigated his credit, court records or looked for evidence of his stability. My mother would always tell me, "Peace of mind is priceless." It gives great comfort to know what the future may hold. The thought never crossed Barbara's mind.

It is a compelling argument that we should make decisions on faith and not on evidence. It invokes some implied rule that a relationship that begins without trust is somehow wrong or fated to fail. I'd prefer to have both faith and the evidence to guide my choices and future decisions. I'm certain Barbara would have still married him if she had this knowledge but she would have been more informed about their financial future.

I cannot say that I am completely free of any hope-based decision making. Barbara's lesson came well before I had doled out thousands of dollars in "good faith" loans to family, friends, and that category of individuals known as new acquaintances. The ones I had known for less than two years or so. These loans had been given out freely based on the hope of repayment. Even trust at that point seemed to be a bit of a stretch considering some of these people had previous loans owed to me that still had not been repaid. So, I knew I couldn't trust them, but I held out hope that if they cared about me or our friendship, they would repay it.

The thing that we must begin to understand is that these people either had good intentions to keep their word or did not have good intentions. What was important was they saw a target or opportunity for their need, someone who was a willing participant, and by asking for help these opportunists had nothing to lose.

Evidence is a Powerful Medicine

Some of the most shocking and revealing examples come from Internet dating. I wonder what percentage of people actually do background checks on these strangers who they let into their homes and browse through their private lives with the click of a mouse.

I enjoy telling the story of my friend Katrina who at the age of thirty-one, was now past her goal of having a baby by thirty. She turned from speed dating to the Internet and investigates everyone she has an interest in.

"It's premature, but it gives me peace of mind," she says.

Her due diligence has paid off in at least one case. After going on a couple of dates with a real estate investor, she took down his tag number only to find the Mercedes 500 SL he was driving was registered in his ex-girlfriend's name. She later discovered that his girlfriend was asking for the car back because he had not made a payment in months. This was the agreement.

"If I had been more diligent, I would have seen the vehicle registration and paperwork in his glove compartment, but I'm not a snooper," Katrina said.

She explained that if she had thought anything was odd, she would have asked to see his driver's license. That was normal and most guys have no problem with that. After all, it is the risk of the Internet. "If he refused, it would have raised questions and caution on my part," Katrina finished.

The information from the investigation is not to help you bail out, but to ask the right questions and then decide on how to proceed.

Today's women have a lot to protect, including their family, job, their life, and present and future children. They are realizing proper investigation is liability insurance for the future.

What is Your Choice?

To be smart is to know that repeating the same behaviors is not progress. To be intelligent is to understand that not everyone is capable of giving the required amount of effort. Manage yourself accordingly. (#DIVAreality)

Delusion, denial, self-sabotage, and other distortions of reality have no place in intelligent living. Situations constantly change and it is up to you to acknowledge the moment for what it is and make decisions that appreciate and take into account the gift of freedom that comes through reality. Hope is sometimes a false positive. It doesn't override reality or make it better than it is. Take what you need as an opportunity to learn and grow.

Five Tips to Managing Expectations

1. Be realistic. Expect nothing and plan for the best *and* the worst.
2. Be prepared to walk away with minimal losses.
3. Show compassion and understanding but guard yourself against false hope.
4. Acknowledge your role in the relationship, when you better understand your and others expectations the relationship may change.
5. People change as situations change, mature and are tested. Ask more questions than give demands.

Personal Space

Noun: the physical space immediately surrounding someone, into which any encroachment feels threatening or uncomfortable to them.

The distance from another person at which one feels comfortable when talking to or being next to that other person.

Invisible boundaries surrounding the individual's body, which is maintained in relation to others.

Synonyms: personal distance.

Our personal space is our comfort zone. It's the physical space, social space, or public space between us and others and is determined by our emotional center or level of intimacy toward each other, the situation, or the environment. Take care to protect and honor that space.

16
LOVE IS NOT A GUARANTEE

"Don't try to comprehend with your mind. Your [our]minds are very limited. Use your intuition."—Madeleine L'Engle

Lora is a twenty-eight-year-old nonprofit fundraiser from Detroit who seeks help to bring positive energy back into her life and a better understanding of a recent onset of self-doubt she felt was holding her back. Her story is important because it illustrates the value of championing yourself and acknowledging your individual gifts within and outside of relationships with others.

LORA

I've only told this story to few people because it frightens me, but there is something too valuable in it for me to allow it to go unspoken. If anything, it taught me to listen to my heart, to pay attention to the meaning of symbols and patterns that reveal themselves. I also learned to add meaning and context to questions, and to self-authenticate my own personal power and the gift of knowledge through intuition.

2003 was a painful year, although, it began with change and optimism for the future. I was having the time of my life as a new college graduate living in a new city with a new fabulous job and no one to tell me what to do or when to do it. For the first time, I felt free to be a complete loafer and contribute nothing to society if I so chose. It was going to be all about me for a change.

Well, the time it took to write that statement was about the same amount of time it took for that feeling of exhilaration to vanish. Between 2003-2005 would be my worst years. The climate for a single, free-spirited woman to blissfully explore the world was suddenly not very good.

It was one bad news story after another centered on domestic violence cases and men killing women. Three local women were killed by their spouses or significant others within weeks of each other. Nationally, there was a well-publicized case of a missing pregnant woman who her unfaithful husband was eventually convicted of murdering so that he could start a new life with the woman with whom he was living a double life.

Despite all of the bad news and feelings of unease, I did have one thing to look forward to that year, my cousin's wedding. Regan was my hero, a corporate vixen who at twenty-seven, had launched a successful Internet brand and was traveling the world as a corporate celebrity.

She loved the people of Central and South America. Most recently, she lived in Colombia for some time and within the past year had moved back to her hometown, built her dream home and had started a new life with her fiancé. Regan had worked hard to build her company into a social media and technology empire. We were all excited. This would be her first marriage.

We had planned a day together after not seeing each other in more than five years. My last correspondence came in the form a photo from a café in Panama City, Panama. She was sitting with friends along the locks of the Panama Canal. She looked happy and carefree. I followed her on social media like an adoring fan.

Regan's fiancé greeted me at the door.

"Hello, I'm Lora. It's so nice to finally meet you." Greg responded with a firm smile and handshake to match. I surmised his perfect teeth were quality veneers. It was apparent from his choice to wear a fitted, cotton blue T-shirt that he worked out and was proud to show off the results.

He was handsome and stood about 6'2" tall. She said he was in sales.

I entered the foyer of a beautifully furnished home, a clear display of Regan's eclectic style. The Victorian furniture with the wood carvings and plush prints complemented the accents of art and collectibles from all over the world that were carefully displayed around the room. It was an entry way that could easily double as a gallery. I imagined there would be many parties and social gatherings held to celebrate an upcoming wedding and showers celebrating the birth of smart and curious children.

"So what's your profession?" Greg asked while walking me into the living room that featured a long winding staircase.

I chuckled and gave away my sense of amusement at the question and then confusion. Didn't he know we were a blue collar family and proud of it? Most people in our family and the community Regan and I grew up in were grateful for an occupation much less a profession.

"I'm a fundraiser for a local university, and you?"

"I'm a salesman," he replied.

I waited for more. Nothing else was offered.

"Well, I suppose that could be a profession or an occupation," I said rather smartly.

His eyes suddenly diverted to something over my shoulder and I felt a tap behind my ear. A smile smeared itself across my face. I turned to my cousin and saw a familiar smile and loving eyes. We embraced and unknowing spun ourselves in a whirlwind of circles, screaming in excitement all the way. It had been years and certainly time to catch up.

"So where's the ring?"

Regan proudly held out her hand to show off a four-carat diamond ring.

I gasped and stood silent unable to speak.

Her eyes were beaming with joy and anxious energy as she waited for me to say the obvious, that I loved it. But, I didn't. The gasp wasn't an impulsive response from the presence of something brilliant and beautiful, it was quite the opposite.

One of the benefits of being from a family of modest means was both the necessity and the opportunity to work yourself through college without the luxury of choice. If I was offered a job, I took it and made the best of it. I had been a cocktail waitress before I was of legal drinking age. I worked at a call center selling expanded Medicare plans to unassuming senior citizens. I sold newspapers, and yes, I had worked in a jewelry store. I knew diamonds and what I saw in front of me was a diamond, but of the poorest quality possible, so poor that it was even visible to the untrained eye. I couldn't find a clear area on which to focus. I felt sadness and pain.

There was something happening here that I didn't yet understand.

Despite the visible flaws, Regan behaved as if she was incapable of seeing anything wrong. It gave more meaning to the phrase "love is blind." Any person, even a child could see the white specks and zigzag lines resembling a shattered window that had been dropped on the floor.

I realized then there was no way she was incapable of seeing it. That wasn't the point.

I said it was pretty and asked how many carats. She stood there smiling in an "I know this ring is hideous" sort of way but please accept it as I did. After all, her fiancé was standing there in the home she built and he had already moved in.

Although Regan and I were six years apart, she felt like a godmother to me. We knew each other's childhood secrets. She had worked through college as a stripper and exotic dancer. She was smart and had shifted to building a career when she landed her first job with a global package delivery company. Her vocabulary consisted of words like global supply chain and international business markets when I was writing papers on the greatest conflicts in American history. I never asked why she made her choices. I only listened when she chose to share. I didn't know if he knew.

I didn't know what to make of my cousin's fiancé. What I knew for certain was the ring was not an investment in someone's future. On the contrary, it signified someone who had no intentions of ever investing in the relationship. The ring was worthless and worst of all, the lack of care in hiding this fact revealed an even greater lack of respect or appreciation for my cousin who had to look into the eyes of everyone who knew her and feign love and worth in something that was worthless. It spoke to his feelings toward her. Although I did not know him, I did not question her feelings toward him. They were genuine.

For me it revealed something very frightening. At the moment I saw it, his presence began to feel like a lingering sickness. There was a turning point I couldn't describe. I felt ill.

I thought to myself, *He's going to kill her within a year.* The thought escaped my mind so freely and so unexpectedly that I waited in horror for the monster in my head to reveal itself. I didn't know where this was coming from. I felt strongly that he hated her. That's what I saw, that's what I felt when I looked into that huge flawed ring.

For weeks, I was tortured by nagging guilt of these self-admissions and wrestled with the thought of telling my cousin how I felt. Eventually, I pushed myself away from the idea. The only way it could be true is if it happened. I reasoned that I was not a psychic; therefore, it could not be true. I also knew that if something were to happen, she wouldn't do anything about it except to allow it to happen. This is what wives do when they want to believe in eternal love, I thought to myself? That is what we had been taught—to be obedient, to be kind and to be selfless.

That was my excuse, for not revealing my unconventional source of concern.

When I left my cousin in the hands of that man, there was one final self-admission. The next time I would see her, she would be dead.

I heard the news that Regan was married from an e-mail. They decided that they wanted to bring in the New Year as husband and wife. I was sure there wouldn't be a wedding and was never notified of a date.

Over the next few months, I would hear family rumors that Regan was in an abusive relationship. She was not traveling anymore and her company seemed to have been turned over to her employees to run. There was talk that she had signed everything over to her husband.

Yes, I thought, she would do this as a symbol of her unconditional love and devotion to him. She wanted so much to be a good and submissive wife.

Several months later Regan became terribly ill and was diagnosed with a rare form of multiple sclerosis. I sent her a get well card and called several times without receiving an answer or returned call. Family members were seeing less of her as well. Our grandmother lived about an hour away in the home where our parents were raised. Regan had chosen to build her home in the nearest county so that she could spend more time with family. Everyone was beginning to worry; surely the honeymoon phase was over.

One morning, I decided to drive the four hours to her home, stopping once to pick up our grandmother as the excuse for her to answer the door.

"Surely they wouldn't turn NeNe away," I thought.

It was a Sunday when she was more likely to be home. We gave her a courtesy call five minutes out and left a message. Greg called back immediately.

"She can't see you today, she's very ill," he said. I knew this and wondered why it mattered. Her illness wasn't contagious and we were family. The image of a sick and unkempt cousin and grandchild wasn't an issue in the least. We both persisted and in five minutes we were on her doorstep.

Greg met us at the door. It was brief and uncaring. We would not be allowed to see her. We left with the promise that she would call us. A week later, I received a note in the mail from Regan. She apologized for not seeing us. She never called.

Two years from the start of that fateful premonition, and a year from that first bout of sickness, I attended Regan's funeral. She was twenty-nine years old and had no children. He had three children from a previous marriage. In the end, she had signed everything over to him. Our family was shocked. I felt regret. Was there anything I could have done?

I never met the man before that first meeting nor had I inquired much about him. I wanted my cousin's happiness to be the memory I took away from my visit that day. But my fears came true. The ring had said it all, but offered little evidence for such a fatal prediction. The rumors continued months after Regan's death, my grandmother mentioned that she had once seen poison on the kitchen counter and questioned why it was near food. No one ever questioned her diagnosis or her death. It was some sort of code, something that family just didn't do.

Regan was now part of that growing list of women who were lost in the culture of abuse and shame. What was exceptional about all of the women who died that year was how beautiful and talented they were. I admit that I am the first to cringe when someone comments on how beautiful a victim was, as if the victims who are not attractive have less value and demand less compassion. What I do know is that beauty inside and out is a mark of what many of us strive to be as people. But for those individuals who hand out abuse and inflict pain, beauty or lack of beauty is not a factor; it is irrelevant to a person living a life of deep delusion and selfishness.

Each day I think about the stolen voices of these heroines and how much they wanted to be independent, successful and loved. These tragic stories of our sisters, daughters and mothers have changed my life. The answers, I find, are right in front of me. Today, I am compelled to stop and listen to their stories rather than turn the channel. They all tell me, beg me, not to cry but to listen. They teach and inspire me to be better by using my inner strength as a guide toward what is good and to seek fully the answers to what I had dared to question.

Each story inspires me to think of the possibility or hope that there is a way of seeing past my own limitations, my own perspectives, and the rules that blind and bind us from saving ourselves and perhaps others. The world is not as we see it; it is as society sees us. And for that reason, we must be honest with the implications of the reality we are dealt.

Love guarantees nothing. It doesn't guarantee parental care and protection, it doesn't guarantee safety and security from the one we most love any more than what it guarantees from a stranger. There is also no guarantee of self-love. We purposely hurt ourselves without just cause or reason. I wonder if Regan lacked self-love.

The answer is to listen and to look deeply into the authentic moments of yourself and others. You must search for that authenticity and appreciate its fragile state. When it begins to crack and lose its clarity, don't be afraid to let it go.

What is Your Choice?

To be smart is to know that loves comes in many forms and degrees of expression. It is subject to shift and change or may stay steadfast. To be intelligent is to understand that we cannot control or help anyone who is committed to self-destruction. No matter how deep is the love. (#DIVAloveisnotaguarantee)

Intuition is a powerful sixth-sense that must be considered in all decisions, whether or not we decide to use it to make the final choice is our call. Our decisions and behaviors and the acceptance of helpful or hurtful behaviors of others toward us frame our future.

Nine Thoughts to Manage Love and Loss

1. Expect nothing.
2. Give everything.
3. Speak from the mind and soul.
4. See from the heart.
5. Challenge limiting beliefs and values.
6. Judge nothing.
7. Appreciate the moment.
8. Value self-love.
9. Start again.

17

BET ON FEAR

"Always go with the choice that scares you the most..." — *Carolyn Myss*

This is a commentary on fear, which along with limiting or irrational beliefs, seems to have the biggest influence on our ability to progress and live our fullest life. It is a challenge worth taking on because the results are limitless, freeing and moves us one more step toward gaining intelligence.

It is my opinion that fear is learned and can therefore be unlearned. But, I am not a psychologist, nor have I explored the body of research on motivation and fear. However, I do think I have enough life experience, coupled with the experiences my friends have shared, to know that the root of much of our fear seems to come from external sources. Sometimes our parents, teachers, clergy, and other well-meaning the people around us exaggerate life in order to "keep us safe." What they are often doing is introducing fear into our minds. Once we reach adulthood, we are left to manage it on our own. Eventually we waste valuable time and opportunities before we understand that we can rein it in.

I often wonder would happen if we had no fear. What would our lives be like if the concept of fear didn't exist? I have seen it in temporary situations. It could be a man rushing out to save a child about to be hit by a car or someone fighting to save a person's life. In these situations there seems to be a temporary lapse of fear overcome by a strong sense of love, selflessness, or empathy. When we consider a life devoid of fear we could do whatever we're passionate about, no matter the outcome. That is the road map of life without fear.

I overcame the fear of water by a combination of embarrassment and will. I overcame flying because it was a condition of hiring for a new job. I wanted this position so badly that I was determined to overcome any obstacle to get it. I began researching accident data on flying versus other methods of transportation and was pleased to find flying was actually much safer than driving. This was reaffirmed in every statistic I could find. My fear was assuaged through motivation, the need for security, and will. After conquering it I accepted the job offer.

Fear is a powerful sedative. It freezes us into paralysis at worst and can slow us down to a snail's pace at best. The middle ground is delay. The most common forms of fear include those that come with change, trying something new, and fear of failure. Fear also drives us to behave in irrational and harmful ways resulting in loss of quality of life and mental anguish.

Employees fear jobs will be lost due to the implementation of new technology. Nations fear roads and transportation systems may fail such as a bridge collapse or a levee break. As a leadership researcher, fear in organized systems such as organizations, communities and social orders are associated with feelings and anxiety brought on by the perception that something familiar and comforting will suddenly change. As a confident and empowered leader, it will be your responsibility to support change while reducing anxiety and fear.

Fear is a political tool that can be used to motivate others in directions that promise to remove it. Fear causes revolutions and revolts. The Salem Witch trials were based on fear. Today, we have strict governance and civil rights policies designed to control the extreme behavior expressed by people when fear is nurtured through formal institutions and cultural practices.

Fear will lead you if you don't take the reins and lead it to its end. That starts with addressing your internal and external motivations that inform your beliefs. What is important to understand about fear is how these affect not only your life, but also your career. For example, this can be refusing to accept a job in another city because you don't know anyone there. Or it could mean refusing an assignment as team leader because it requires you to travel by plane. It could also be failing to submit an application because you were afraid they wouldn't hire you because of your nationality. Fear will get you fired when you allow lack of knowledge or ignorance of other people guide your language and behavior.

Online communities define fear as a mind killer and a paralyzing emotion that takes over your mind causing negative thinking, anger, and even more fear They also refers to fear as "a waste of your time caused by lack of familiarity with the experience." I use these definitions because they seem to come from real and personal experiences in contrast to the abstract definitions offered by dictionaries. For example, a definition offered by Merriam-Webster defines fear as "an unpleasant often strong emotion caused by anticipation or awareness of danger."

The most important lesson for overcoming fear is to better understand what drives it. The motivation to overcome fear is critical because of the power it holds and the effect it can have on the minds and behaviors of individuals, groups, and nations. Fear will drive us unless we drive it.

Fear can manifest in many situations. I imagine that, like me, you will not master the goal of eliminating oncoming feelings of fear, but will come to recognize it for what it is and ignore it. My first sense of oncoming fear is delay, then pressure, and then anxiety. I'm working on stopping it at delay. Online communities are correct; fear is a time killer as much as it is a mind killer.

Managing fear is a sign of someone who is highly self-aware and emotionally intelligent Keep moving and don't let fear delay your success. Learned or taught fears can be overcome if we wish. However, the most dangerous fears are the ones that take away our peace of mind, cause unhealthy behaviors or anxieties, and keep us stuck in life.

Popular polls show that some of the most common fears include public speaking, death, failure, rejection, heights, and talking to people of the opposite sex. One of the most comprehensive studies on fear comes from Chapman University and their annual study of American Fears. The 2016 study of about 79 different types of fears measured a broad range of topics Americans fear such as disasters, technology, terrorism, the paranormal, conspiracies, and even clowns. The top three fears of 2016 included corrupt government officials (60.6%), a terrorist attack (41%), and not having enough money for the future (38.5). The full list can be accessed at:

https://blogs.chapman.edu/wilkinson/2016/10/11/americas-top-fears-2016/

What is Your Choice?

To be smart is to know that fear and stalled growth are synonyms. One does not exist without the other. To be intelligent is to understand that you must leverage fear to bring about forward movement and progress, which champions new and innovative thinking. (#DIVAbetonfear)

If there is one thing that is certain, it is that you can bet on fear. Overcoming that fear comes with maturity and a personal obligation to reassess childhood beliefs and teachings. What was first instilled to provide guidance and structure must now evolve to meet a higher level of social inspiration and global understanding that leads to personal growth, fulfillment and lasting happiness.

Six Tips to Overcome Fear

1. Don't overthink.
2. List your pros and cons for not making a choice. What will you gain? What will you lose? How much or what percentage is rooted in fear?
3. Look to the opportunities.
4. Talk through your fear with a confidante.
5. Seek inspiration through leaders, influencers and decision makers.
6. Take one step forward. Then take another. Don't overthink.

18
GET A PERSONAL COACH

"Everybody needs a coach." — Eric Schmidt, COO Google & Bill Gates

This is part two of my story, which tells of my experiences with the professions that make up psychiatry, counseling, therapy, and coaching. The distinction between these forms of professional support is important to understand. The biggest distinction is that a coach is an equal partner in a healthy relationship designed to help you overcome challenges to what you desire in life. Rather than give advice, coaches ask powerful questions to help you discover your own answers. We are advocates and champions to assist you in creating the life you desire. Coaching uses positive psychology, solutions-focused, and strengths-based methods proven effective for personal and professional development.

BROOKS

In Chapter 1, I told the story of Coach Dailey, my high school coach who was the first person to tell me I had no common sense. If that was my first epiphany about intelligence and our capacity to think, then my second epiphany would be the discovery that intelligence could be improved through development of knowledge, skills and experiences.

I was well into obtaining my master's degree and had nearly ten years of professional experience behind me when I first understood the term "coach" had broader meaning than an athletic coach. I had been moving up the career ladder and accomplishing my goals; however, I was disappointed in how long it was taking and my inability to focus on one thing at a time. To further complicate my path of self-development, I decided to change careers. After exploring my options, I came across an exciting discovery. I had the choice to have a new coach—a personal and professional coach.

Professional coaching was described to me as a partnership between a coach and a client wherein the coach provides a safe and open, nonjudgmental space that facilitates discussions that would allow me to think through my own problems and maximize my personal and professional potential. The outcome is more self-awareness and a better understanding of my own life decisions and the motivations that inspire them. The brochure from my HR representative offered several definitions but the one that resonated with me was the concept of coaching as a proven method of "...challenging and supporting people in achieving higher levels of performance while allowing them to bring out the best in themselves and those around them."[xxv]

The prospect of having that one-on-one relationship with someone who could challenge my thinking was exciting. I'd never worked with a coach before, and I was hopeful that it would give me what had been missing in my previous discussions with counselors and therapists. They had been helpful in addressing my specific needs, but there seemed to be a disconnection between me and my problem. I wanted someone who could focus on me. A professional coach would offer a trained ear to help me to understand my authentic self and set a long-term course for greater achievement, success and accountability.

On those three occasions when I had used professional help, one was as a student, another as an employee, and last as a member of a newly blended family. These experiences were important in bringing to my attention increased awareness that led to life-changing guidance. Each time I learned something valuable about myself. I was happy to know that there are people in place to assist you in getting out of a downward spiral and can help to redirect your trajectory. Unfortunately, these prior experiences were short-term situations that when corrected gave you the confidence to continue on unaided.

My first experience with a therapist was in my last year of college. It started when my brother, who told me I was "book smart" told my mother that I had an eating disorder and was "trying to kill myself."

Yes, those were his words and I'll never forget them. In his defense, we are a brash speaking crowd, no words are left unsaid. We were raised to tell the truth, no filter.

But his observation and harsh proclamation frightened me because I *had* lost a lot of weight and I hadn't noticed. I was overwhelmed with coursework, job interviews, and lack of sleep due to an emotionally draining and tense collegiate environment. It was the time of the Gainesville student murders and most recently the insanity of the Florida State University student murders. I felt sick and frustrated because I couldn't lose those last few pounds I wanted before going on interviews. I still get mad thinking about it, but, he was right.

I must have mentioned these feelings to my mother because before long my younger brother Billy called to confront me.

"Brooks, what's this about? Mother says you're trying to kill yourself."

I was not the least bit shocked. I was used to my mother's drama as well.

"No, I'm on a new diet," I told him. "I'm cutting out meat and I've been feeling a bit faint." I became a chatterbox when I spoke with my brothers. It was a habit formed from growing up between two boys. Each of us spoke in run-on sentences, afraid that if we stopped, someone else would start and we'd never get a chance to finish. Billy was the youngest. My matter-of-fact brother was the oldest. Billy was the sensitive one.

"Okay, if you feel faint maybe you should eat more," he said. I could almost see the "duh" expression on his face as we spoke on the phone.

I thought, *Why don't you just kiss my ass and shut the hell up Billy.*

What I said was, "You're right."

I promised him that I would go to the doctor the next day. I then hung up feeling moody and anxious. Maybe it was because I felt exposed. Why can't they just let me run my own life? I wondered.

As promised, I went to the see the doctor. After a brief examination and what seemed to be many related and unrelated questions, the doctor referred me to a therapist. I thought she was overly concerned.

Once I met with the therapist, I realized I had been a bit depressed and stressed out. I didn't realize it. The talk about my class schedule, upcoming job interviews, and timing of the new diet put it all into perspective. I appreciated their help. Sometimes we do need an independent party or an alarmist big brother to bring us to our senses and help us get out of our own way.

After that impressionable experience, I developed, over the years, a habit of buying friends one hour therapy sessions as holiday gifts. To me it was the most valuable thing I could give. They would have an impartial, knowledgeable person to talk out their problems with and discover the trigger they were too close to see clearly. I do believe it made many of them emotionally stronger and more confident. Today, I purchase life, business, and career coaching sessions

The second time I called for professional help was to address workplace conflict. I relocated to Philadelphia for a new job and had been there for less than a year before I met my future husband. It was clear there would be no turning back. I loved my new job and the new role I was in; however, he lived in another state. My boss, who was a very possessive man, wouldn't hear of it. For him it was a loyalty issue. For me it was a love issue.

Following a very contentious meeting where I was made to feel selfish and untrustworthy, I lost the desire to come back to work. After sitting in bed for the next three days, I called the employee assistance program and was immediately referred to a psychiatrist. I remember her first question.

"What's the problem?"

She was a nice middle-aged woman with unkempt hair and an organized mess of an office. But, it was comfortable.

"I don't want to go back to work," I answered.

Our conversation continued over three one-hour sessions. Her final question summed it up.

"Why would you want to work for a boss who is so selfish?"

I couldn't answer her question with any confidence or clear meaning.

The next day, I called and resigned.

This counselor and coach gave me what I had been missing, an advocate who was able to assuage my doubt and ignite my desire to have a full and rewarding life at home and work.

The third and most recent time I sought professional help was after a family holiday conflict, which resulted in so much anger, bitterness, anxiety and confusion that I felt I needed an independent party to help me sort it out. I was now dealing with teenage stepchildren. Having none of my own, I was completely void of ideas about how it was supposed to work. But, my concern was also deeper than that, I felt extreme guilt because I didn't care if it worked or not. I felt horrible about it.

I called the spousal support program for my job. I was assigned to a family therapist who I met with over thirteen one-hour sessions. It was an interesting transformation. I realized that although I may not care, I did want to have positive relationships with my stepdaughters. Part of the responsibility of having a positive relationship was to reach out more and communicate. Our distance was an underlying roadblock, but proactively reaching out to engage them was mostly my responsibility. I decided to call them on a regular basis, something I had not done before and the communication has improved our level of understanding. My role is to be a mentor, to offer guidance and support when I can, nothing more is required. My feelings of guilt are long gone.

I learned that there is a difference between therapy, counseling, coaching and even mentoring. I make this point because counselors and therapists are helpful for specific needs that are associated with mental health and psychological counseling; however, they are far from being personal and professional coaches.

Everyone Needs a Personal Coach

Not everyone needs a therapist, or a counselor, but everyone needs a personal coach.

One of the best advocates for professional coaching is Bill Gates and Eric Schmidt, chairman and COO of Google, who said that some of the best advice he received as a new COO was "you need a coach." Schmidt said in an interview, "Every famous athlete, every famous performer has somebody who is a coach." Schmidt described his coaching experience as one of trust and improved perspective.

"One thing that people are never good at is seeing themselves as others see them," Schmidt said. "I realized I could trust him [the coach] and that he could help me with perspective, I decided this was a great idea..."[xxvi]

If CEOs, performers and athletes have professional and personal coaches and praise their work, why is it that the rest of us know so little about them? Why should only they have that edge?

The coaching profession has grown exponentially over the years in executive offices and upper management. It is now trickling town to middle managers and employees across all levels of the organization. The need for coaching will continue to increase as smart, self-directed employees and employers benefit from these services.

In fact, some professional coaching has broadened into many areas that fall under the general description of life coaching. They include niches such as leadership coaching, executive coaching, wellness coaching, public speaking and communication coaching, small business and entrepreneurship coaching and many more.

My first experience with coaching was nearly fifteen years ago, which now seems like a lifetime. I was a graduate student. That was when I was introduced to a leadership coach who helped me to assess my strengths, weaknesses and talents and then develop an individual action plan and goals to help me to focus on developing my leadership abilities. Early on, one of my greatest challenges was self-confidence. One of my key goals was to focus on identifying the barriers to gaining self-confidence and creating or identifying specific exercises, tools and programs that can be tailored to address different situations and environments that are confidence killers. For example, in my case, fear and self-doubt have been common barriers to sustaining confidence and once it is achieved in that specific area, another scenario can just as quickly take it away.

My coach worked with me to understand the traits of a transformational leader and how to self-coach myself out of fear at the onset and continuously improve my leadership development skills. "Never give up" was my career mantra. It has since changed to something along the lines of "Now or never." But, my problem has not been giving up, but rather the challenge of overcoming the accumulation of guilt brought on by self-doubt from starting and restarting. My coach helped me to clarify, put the doubt behind me and move forward.

One thing that I came to understand about leadership is that it involves the ability to motivate and inspire others to be leaders by empowering them to also develop their talents and abilities to self-lead and self-manage. I realized that I had been a selfish task manager who spent little time developing and inspiring others. Today that is one of my greatest strengths.

The personal coaching process is one of inquiry and advocacy to help you make changes that enhance your effectiveness and develop a course of action to achieve your goals. Coaching is action oriented, solutions-focused and future-focused.

Cases of Women & Successful Coaching Outcomes

I recently had an opportunity to attend a coaching panel of professional women leaders from the healthcare industry, railroad industry, business entrepreneurship sector, and higher education. The hosting organization was sponsoring a Wisdom Circle event where clients spoke of their experiences with leadership coaching, business coaching, and life coaching professionals. It was a great learning experience and throughout the session I was fixated on two women in particular.

One was a very tall and thin executive, I'll call her Sandra. She was around 5'10" and about 140 pounds. She had short curly-blonde hair that gave a sense of fun to her simple but tailored look. By simple, I mean that she wore no jewelry with the exception of button earrings. Nothing was in excess. Although she had broken through the glass ceiling of one of the area's oldest railroad companies, she couldn't have done it without the help of her coach. She has since left the company, but not before being awarded several pay raises to match increasing responsibilities and a long overdue promotion.

Reflecting back she realized that the culture of the organization was that of a "good old boys" club. The employees were so glad to simply be included that they didn't even ask to be paid what they were worth. They were simply thankful for what they got.

Work-life challenges that Sandra's coach helped her to think through and overcome included, knowing how to "communicate up," working with a "toxic boss," "nurturing a potential leader," "feeling stuck," and gaining "confidence."

To effectively communicate up the chain of command means that employees must create their own channel of communication to ensure leaders are aware of their interests and needs. One role of a leader is to identify and nurture others with leadership potential. An important aspect of nurturing potential leaders includes an improved understanding of organizational culture and how to use informal channels of communication to get their messages to the decision makers. This may be difficult when working with a toxic boss who is often associated with micromanaging or engages in intimidating, overbearing and unproductive behavior such as bullying, sabotage, and arrogance.

People working with toxic bosses or those who work in jobs where they feel unsatisfied may begin to feel stuck or trapped in their roles. This feeling also applies to our personal lives when we feel we are not living the life we desire and have yet to find solutions to get us on track.

Confidence is gained when people increasingly demonstrate a desired result leading to trust in their or another's abilities.

After hearing her speak, it reconfirmed that I had found my personal platform to help others to reach personal and professional fulfillment.

What all the panelists demonstrated was that the glass ceiling was half our responsibility to enable, but 100 percent of our responsibility to overcome.

It was clear, that the panelists would not be in their leadership positions, with the salary they demanded that was often higher than initially offered, if not for their professional coaches whom they all thanked and acknowledged. I was empowered by their life stories, which we all should hear sooner in our careers rather than later.

The event was very inspiring and I saw this particular panel as a public service opportunity for young women leaders. Not only did they speak of how professional coaching helped them, but how it helped them to overcome the particular challenges women silently endure in the workplace. A coach is an advocate for goal and action-oriented, solutions-focused change. Coaching is a proven method to improve your professional coping skills through self-development and self-efficacy gained by transforming your weaknesses into strengths and your strengths into assets.

Coaches use a range of tools, methodologies and assessments that include personal inventories that measure or identify ranges of personality and leadership styles.

In my coaching practice, the Enneagram is one of many tools we use to help individuals explore why they have certain points of view. It is their way of seeing the world and how it may relate to their choices, behaviors and beliefs. Like the Core Motivation chart included in Chapter 3, the Enneagram seeks to identify our way of thinking, sensing and feeling. It helps us to explore our emotional compass. By acknowledging these individual differences we are able to direct our emotional maturity and let go of limiting beliefs. The Enneagram is also helpful to understand others and why they perceive or do things in certain ways or situations. The key is to better understand yourself and how your traits may be holding you back.

What is Your Choice?

To be smart is to know you need a coach. To be intelligent is to understand your needs and make the investment to overcome them when you can't do it alone. Add a coach to your wisdom circle and begin to manifest the outcomes you want. (#DIVAcoach)

I was raised to be nice. I was raised to be kind and giving. I was raised to trust. After giving away all of that energy, I questioned what was left to give to myself and to make living my life a priority. Everyone needs a personal coach to help them to release old demons and find a fresh new path that writes your authentic story.

Seven Tips to Working with a Personal Coach

1. Know your area of need such as work challenges, personal life or career development.
2. Be honest and open.
3. Do the work. Be accountable to yourself and the process.
4. Be mindful of the experience. Appreciate the small accomplishments.
5. Recognize the "aha" moments.
6. Celebrate every moment.
7. Pause to recognize and acknowledge success.

LEADERSHIP SELF-INVENTORY (BLANK FORM)

WHO AM I MOST LIKELY TO BE? LEADERSHIP SELF-INVENTORY Name:					
Strengths	Weaknesses	Talents		Passion (motivation)	Fears (motivation)
Personality (Inner-Self)				Persona Public-Self)	
Behavior/Soft Skills to Acquire (opportunities for self-development)		Actions for Self-Development		Timeline
Self-Assessments taken		When taken			Comments/Action

MY LEADERSHIP SELF-INVENTORY EXAMPLE

WHO AM I MOST LIKELY TO BE?				
LEADERSHIP SELF-INVENTORY: Dr. Dunbar				
Strengths	**Weaknesses**	**Talents**	**Passion** (motivation)	**Fears** (motivation)
Intellect	Introversion	Relator		
Emotional Stability	Sensitivity	Achiever		
Social Assertiveness	Abstractness	Includer		
Open-Mindedness	Dutifulness	Strategic		
		Learner		
Personality (Inner-Self)			**Persona (Public-Self)**	
Behavior/Soft Skills to Acquire (opportunities for self-development)		**Actions for Self-Development**		**Timeline**
1. Extroversion (Public Speaking)		1. Enroll in Toastmasters		1. 30 days

Self-Assessments taken	When taken	Comments/Action
1. StrengthsFinder 2.0	1. May 2016	1. see talents/ask HR for help/resources

19

INSPIRATION

"My mother told me to be a lady. And for her, that meant to be your own person, be independent." — The Notorious RBG

Dawn is a twenty-seven-year-old banquet and sales manager from Philadelphia who contacted me because she was seeking a coach and personal champion who would challenge her to grow and take action to achieve what she wanted in life. Her story is important because it illustrates how personal challenges can be reframed to anchor future goals and design action steps that create the positive future we want. It also shows how the loss of a friend can inspire us to live out our dreams as a way of carrying on their legacy.

DAWN

I made it to my twenty-seventh birthday before the word "murder" became part of my life story. I was at work and completely engrossed in a grand opening event. I put in twelve hours that day without a lunch break. "Classics" was a new restaurant and banquet venue located in one of the oldest and most distinguished landmarks in Orlando. This was my first big break as a banquet and sales manager and I wanted it to go well. The city's notables were all juiced with the latest news; it was a very exciting time for me! I felt good about my choice to leave a steady job in healthcare administration to venture out on my own.

"So how are you feeling about the big day?" Meredith asked me.

Meredith had become one of my closest friends since I moved to "The City Beautiful." She encouraged me to put a proposal in to the owners and to my surprise, I got the job. In addition to offering event planning services, I also included event sales assistance.

The meeting with two males and one female partner went extremely well. I wore a sharp, fitted, red business suit with an A-line skirt that stopped two inches above the knees. It was enough to show off my runner's legs. I knew in this business, that appearance and looks were just as, if not more important that skills. Sales really weren't about sales, it was about image. Besides, it didn't hurt to generate some imagination from would-be clients. It wasn't my place to judge the quality or direction of their thoughts. It was a subtle example of how beneficial it could be to have me as part of the company's team of consultants.

I really needed this contract and went in both mentally and physically prepared to exceed any other competitors' offers. I was the complete package.

Meredith was the first person I called when I won the contract. We met at an event sponsored by the local chamber of commerce. I joined immediately after starting my company, Table Runners, Inc. As a new member, the perks were starting to pay off. She was my first "networking" contact that turned into a good lead.

Meredith was a real estate agent, divorced with one teenage daughter. She never spoke of her age but I estimated she was in her mid forties based on her frequent mentions of first, second and third careers. Her early entertainment career included appearances on popular television competition shows before the reality-TV craze became a hit. She was Japanese-

American, petite, and had the most beautiful California-bronzed skin I had ever seen. I envied her for that. She wore her pencil straight, shiny black hair up in a loose bun. Wisps of hair fell around her face and shoulders as if purposely placed there piece by piece. Her makeup was perfectly applied as if she had a personal makeup artist on call for hourly touch-ups. I imagined her secret life was as a millionaire matchmaker. I was sure that she came across as intimidating to anyone who noticed her from across a room. She seemed unapproachable in her perfection. Somehow, I sensed she was aware of this false perception. She had made the first introduction.

Meredith held out her hand for a firm handshake. On her finger was a single two-carat emerald ring and her perfect manicure was a sign of luxury to someone like me, who did her own manicures at home.

That day, Meredith brought lunch.

"Thank goodness food is here," I gasped.

I was starving and hadn't taken the time to thank her properly. It was sushi, light for the occasion, but it would have to do. Meredith was highly perceptive and intuitive. I appreciated that about her and she was never wrong regarding how I was feeling.

"I'm really feeling good about it," I responded to her silent inquiry. "All the publicity materials went out on time and I'm confident RSVPs will start pouring in soon."

"Well, just make sure the Mayor and district commissioner will have their reps there. That's all you'll really need for the entourage to follow."

I smiled. She was right as always, but modest. Not only had she given me her VIP client list, she had also called on her commercial partners and asked that they book any of their special events at the venue on the grand opening. It was going to be a cash cow for the owners and my earnings wouldn't be too shabby either. My contract included a nice commission on any banquets booked or reserved on the day of the opening.

Meredith was becoming a good friend and a mentor. Surely she saw the connection that would follow if she stayed close to me and the owners. There was the potential for real estate clients who would need her expertise.

After a nice chat about strategy and the day's activities, Meredith left for some afternoon property showings. I stayed at the venue until about 7:00 PM and then called it a day. It had been such a good week that I decided a pint of triple chocolate ice cream was more than appropriate for dinner since lunch was a bit light on calories and breakfast was only a bagel.

Home was now a three-bedroom condo. I sold my first house, which I purchased a few years earlier at a loss, but still saved on the spacious 1,200 square foot condo. It was located on the outlying area of a desirable zip code, one with addresses that suggested old money and new commercial development to attract an elite business community.

Home was quiet and serene when I arrived that evening. With the twinkle of lights in the windows of the rows of adjoining quadraplexes, I imagined my extended community of families—all of whom I didn't know—had finished their dinner and were storing purposely proportioned leftovers in the fridge. Soon they'd be spending quality time with their families before retiring for bed.

Now it was my turn to detox from a long day. I prepped for my "me-time" ritual that today would include a pint of nutty chocolate ice cream. It was always too hard when I purchased it from the corner market, so my method included rinsing a large tablespoon with warm water. I then placed a warm blanket on my favorite couch and my comfort zone was complete with the ice cream placed within reach on the coffee table. I would savor the moment.

I headed upstairs for a quick shower to wash away the day. About fifteen minutes later, I returned to the couch, wearing my favorite pink pajamas and slippers. I turned on the TV and opened the tub of ice cream ready to begin my self indulgence. I then curled up on the couch and flipped the channel to watch an old episode of *Frasier*. It always brought a successful end to the day with a much needed laugh.

But something wasn't right. The lead story in a news break flashed a photo of someone I knew well. Though it was an older high school photo, I was certain it was her. I hesitated, and then turned the channel to the local news. My spoon was cool and the tub of chocolate was sweating. Then I saw it. I'd watched news stories of tragedy and loss so many times it was nothing more than an abstract storyline that I heard too often. Today, I couldn't ignore it. The report was about, someone I knew, my friend. She was dead?

But I just spoke with her yesterday? I didn't quite understand what was happening. Immediately I Googled the local news station.

Patricia's name, occupation, and photo were displayed under the words local murder-suicide. My mind searched for answers. Why had they used her high school cheerleading picture? Why would they do this? I didn't understand. I checked my phone. I hadn't missed any calls. There had to be an explanation for this, or there was some kind of mix-up. My mind raced through a Rolodex of current and forgotten friends. Why had no one called me? Wasn't I supposed to see her this weekend? Would I still get the chance to surprise her at one of her charity events?

Then in a moment of heartbreaking disbelief and shock I understood. My friend Patricia was dead. An hour later, at least one question was answered. I called Meredith. She immediately picked up.

"No one knew how to tell you," Meredith said. "You were having such a great day and I just couldn't...I'm so sorry."

Meredith had informed my clients who kept me busy and on site.

Patricia's murder-suicide was the first of three murders that summer. They were all women, brutally and tragically murdered by boyfriends, husbands and fathers. One of the women, like Patricia, was single and childless and had never been married. She was a model. The other was a loving mother and caregiver. All were in the prime of their lives. Patricia was an attorney and wanted to be the state's first female Attorney General. Her colleagues and all of her friends knew it would be just a matter of time before she was. Like Meredith, she was my mentor, but she was also my longtime classmate and friend.

That day changed me. It inspired me from that day forward to try to make a difference. I needed to somehow make up for the ground that had been lost with Patricia's passing. I wanted to do something to commemorate life and her memory and to make others aware of the good she'd done in her life.

Today, we are in the nineteenth year of the celebration of her life. The scholarship created in her name has paid the way for many young women to attend law school. I see her face and her spirit in all of them.

Regardless of the tragedies we face, we must find a way to keep the pace, to not lose ground, on the impact we can make.

What is Your Choice?

To be smart is to know that life comes with heartache and pain. To be intelligent is to understand that this commences a new energy and a new calling that only you can deliver. It's unique to you and can only be born through you. The loss of a sister, family member or friend can inspire us to live out our dreams as a way of carrying on their legacy. Live life without regret and wait for no one, not even the one. That was Dawn's gift to Patricia. (#DIVAinspiration)

Improve yourself and take on opportunities that celebrate and recognize what was to be the change your loved one would have brought to the world. The heart and mind is loss, but not the spirit and the hope that they saw in the world. Choose to carry on and make the difference you and those affected would want to see as part of the legacy circle of life.

Six Tips for Inspiration

1. Dream big and be inspired by the memory of others.
2. Envision a bold and bright future that seems out of reach.
3. Learn from heartache and pain.
4. Think globally.
5. Appreciate life.
6. Find what brings you joy.

CONCLUSION

Diva Decisions is about the power of relationships and our ability to self-determine. You now have the tools to understand how to self-manage and self-lead by increasing your emotional, social, and self-awareness. An important part of this road to self-discovery is an understanding of how to better manage our relationships, whether they are personal—with our family and friends—or in the workplace as a coworker or manager. How you make intelligent choices is contingent on how you can effectively manage and lead yourself and others through the competing realities of what is real and what is perceived. Ultimately, that requires making intelligent choices.

Intelligence demands a high level of awareness of your strengths and skills, the ability to understand the meaning of relationships between people and things, and management of emotional energy coming from you and from others.

Exercising your inherent power of choice begins with self-awareness and self-education. It includes taking control of your own health, wellness, and safety, with as much investment as your education and professional pursuits. You now have the evidence that supports a new way of thinking about personal success and the power of self-driven leadership. It should be clear that the elements that make up your success are broader and deeper than having self-esteem or a mentor or role model to mirror. I want you to continuously remind yourself of the critical importance of knowing that success is hinged upon understanding the social and emotional messages, with underlying meanings, that make up your life. It means developing charismatic, creative, and transformative leadership behaviors that move away from fixed thinking (knowing) to fluid thinking (knowing *and* understanding) that will allow you to more effectively lead yourself and others through life's challenges.

Your first steps are to create your plan to self-actualize, to empower your talents and skills across the four dimensions of your 4D LifeSpace—self, career, relationships, and in your personal space. These are the skills that teachers or academics cannot teach or customize to fit who you are. It is within your power of choice to let go and reframe your thinking, to make better choices, and take the first step toward living a fuller life.

It is my wish that you will use the hashtags in the book to continue the conversations through social platforms. Tell your stories related to each theme or tell us how you were able to get from smart to intelligent. It is my wish that *Diva Decisions* has given you the confidence and skills to make more intelligent choices and fully realize your potential.

LAST WORDS

I want to leave you with this excerpt from *The Golden Notebook* by Doris Lessing. To me it perfectly embodies my thoughts on working women and girls, sexism, gender equity, pay disparity, feminism, gender equality and the 2016 U.S. presidential election results.

"Ideally, what should be said to every child, repeatedly, throughout his or her school life is something like this: 'You are in the process of being indoctrinated. We have not yet evolved a system of education that is not a system of indoctrination. We are sorry, but it is the best we can do. What you are being taught here is an amalgam of current prejudice and the choices of this particular culture. The slightest look at history will show how impermanent these must be. You are being taught by people who have been able to accommodate themselves to a regime of thought laid down by their predecessors. It is a self-perpetuating system. Those of you who are more robust and individual than others will be encouraged to leave and find ways of educating yourself—educating your own judgements. Those that stay must remember, always, and all the time, that they are being moulded and patterned to fit into the narrow and particular needs of this particular society."

ABOUT THE AUTHOR

Dr. V. Brooks Dunbar has spent two decades mentoring and coaching young and professional women. She offers a refreshingly holistic view on personal and career growth, combining practical tips and surefire tools with raw and insightful emotional intelligence. Her global network of affiliations and interests include women's funds, professional business and entrepreneurship institutes, and women in higher education. She was a doctoral fellow of the British Academy of Management and a visiting researcher at Cranfield University School of Management, England. Dunbar earned a doctorate in management with emphasis in organizational crisis leadership and decision making; and a master's degree in public administration with concentration in human resource policy and management.

Dr. Dunbar is a certified Academic Life Coach and holds a Graduate Certificate in Organizational and Leadership Coaching. She is a highly-aware (intuitive) and strategically-oriented leader, mentor, coach, and manager with more than twenty years of knowledge, education, training, and experience gained in the U.S. and abroad. Through her own learning and experiences with business, entrepreneurship, and women's advocacy around the world, she has become a passionate and dedicated advocate for career-focused young women and girls. Her coaching specialty includes student leadership development, managerial leadership, and mindfulness coaching. She uses evidence-based management and evidence-based coaching principles to improve individual, team and organizational leadership performance. She is passionate about people, helping others and promoting life-changing opportunities to help you reach your full potential. Dr. Dunbar is currently the Founder and Lead Coach at The Center for Confidence, LLC. The center provides executive and leadership coaching and other niche coaching services to individuals and organizations. Find her at:

    Author site: www.drvbrooksdunbar.com
    Work: www.TheCenterforConfidence.com
    Facebook @drvbrooksdunbar
    LinkedIn: www.linkedin.com/in/drdunbar
    Instagram:www.instagram.com/drvdunbar

THE CENTER FOR CONFIDENCE

The Center for Confidence LLC (TCFC) is a professional training and leadership development firm providing academic, organizational and leadership life-coaching to students and professionals seeking self-development, performance improvement, and broadened life-skills training. TCFC uses the proprietary 4D Life Skills model incorporating the fourth dimension of life, addressing periods of transformation, resilience, and recovery for purposeful integration of self, career, relationships, and personal space (The 4D Life Skills).

The Center for Confidence provides academic, organizational and leadership coaching, training, and leadership development. We specialize in personal, professional, and leadership development to empower you to realize your true self and bring out your full potential.

Mission: Our mission is to empower every person to gain and sustain confidence to achieve their full life potential.

Vision: Our vision is to instill leadership self-confidence in every individual, from the earliest age, at the earliest opportunity.

IN MEMORIAM

Ms. Robin Lynn Young, Esq.

1965 - 1999

ACKNOWLEDGMENTS

Thank you to the team of Women Owned Small Businesses Enterprises (WOSBE) who helped bring this resource to life. ALane Pearce, Author Coach, Odenton, MD; Morgan S. Taylor, Feminine Wisdom Academy, Austin, TX; and CS Lewis & Publicity, New York. I want to thank Jana Martin of Writing and Editing, Woodstock, NY for starting me on my editorial path and my editor, Carol Taylor who took me to the finish line. Many thanks to Danielle Mathis of Charlotte, NC; A Nuance Art, in New Jersey and Fairburn, GA; and Angela Spears Communication in Jacksonville, FL. Last, but never least, thanks to The Center for Confidence, LLC in Jacksonville, FL.

Also on the journey were Jacksonville-based WOSBEs who gave much needed writers therapy, motivation and promotional support: Dr. Asha Jaleel, Academic Therapy Solutions, Inc.; Tonya Holifield, Boutique 3:16; Marci Cervone, Anam Cara Essentials; Cindy Platt, Grease Rags Clothing Co.; and members of The International Coach Federation First Coast Charter Chapter.

LIST OF TABLES, DIAGRAMS AND CHARTS

Item	Page Number
The Three Skill Approach of Success and Intelligence	31
IQ Scale	41
The Fourr Quadrant Model of Emotional and Social Intelligence	42
Core Motivation Chart	63
Reiss' 16 Basic Desires	68
My Wisdom Circle	86
Maslow's Hierarchy of Needs	124
The Big Five Personality Assessment	143
Cattell's 16 Factor Key for Personality Types	147
Summary of Evidence on Self Esteem	220
Social and Cultural Awareness Bucket List	242
Unconscious and Hidden Bias Questionnaires	245
Leadership Self-Inventory (Blank form)	298
My Leadership Self-Inventory Example	299

LIST OF HASHTAGS

Let's continue the conversation.

#DIVAgetintelligent

#DIVAiqeq

#DIVApower

#DIVAprettyisatalent

#DIVAmakepeace

#DIVAauthenticself

#DIVAownyourpersona

#DIVAquestionauthority

#DIVAtrustbutverify

#DIVAmultiplemes

#DIVAselfpreservation

#DIVAknowyourprice

#DIVAadaptandovercome

#DIVAeliminatejudgment

#DIVAreality

#DIVAloveisnotaguarantee

#DIVAbetonfear

#DIVAcoach

#DIVAinspiration

#DIVADECISIONS

Source: Quotes by Women in Power on Women and Power, located on SlideShare at https://tinyurl.com/nylml9u

READER'S RESOURCES

There are many professional, civic and nonprofit organizations whose missions serve women and girls worldwide. These groups contribute to the social, cultural and leadership development that creative career women need to get from smart to intelligent. Unfortunately, many are unaware of these groups and what they provide to women, families and their local communities. *Can We Talk USA* is the only organization I'm aware of that allows these diverse groups to come together under one umbrella to cross promote and collaborate for the purposes of increasing awareness and strengthening their capacity to do more. *Can We Talk USA* is now on a mission to go global.

Can We Talk collaborative events are scheduled each year in March, to commemorate Women's History Month, and on or near August 26, to commemorate Women's Equality Day. Member events are held year-round and promoted through *Can We Talk's* social media pages. Find us on Facebook@canwetalkjacksonville

Member organizations offer professional development opportunities, provide valuable relationship building platforms, and create lasting social connections that are critical for career progression and success. An example of the member organizations in San Antonio, Texas (Can We Talk SA) include:

Alamo Breast Cancer Foundation
Alpha Home, Inc.
American Association of University Women–San Antonio Branch
American Society of Women Accountants
Annie's List
Association for Women in Communications, Inc.
Bexar County Democratic Women
Bexar County Women's Bar Association
Center for Women in Church and Society
Daughters of Charity Services of San Antonio
Delta Sigma Theta Sorority, Inc.
Dress for Success San Antonio
Esperanza Peace and Justice Center
Executive Women's Golf Association
Family Assistance Crisis Team (FACT)
Family Violence Prevention Services
Federally Employed Women
Financial Women in Texas
Friendship Bridge
Fuerza Unida
Heidi Search Center

Girl Scouts of Southwest Texas
Girls Inc. of San Antonio
Hispanas Unidas
Hispanic Women's Network of Texas- San Antonio Chapter
IMPACT San Antonio
Institute of Texan Cultures
Leadership Texas Alumnae Association
League of Women Voters of the San Antonio Area
Martinez Street Women's Center
Mayor's Commission on the Status of Women
Mujeres Unidas Contra El SIDA
National Association of Professional Mortgage Women
National Association of Women Business Owners
National Coalition of 100 Black Women, S. A. Chapter
National Council of Negro Women
National Organization of Women (NOW)
National Ovarian Cancer Coalition
National Sorority of Phi Delta Kappa, Inc.
Network Power/Texas
P.E.A.C.E. Initiative
Pan American Round Tables of Texas
Planned Parenthood South Texas
Planned Parenthood South Texas Votes
Rape Crisis Center

SLEW Wellness Center
San Antonio College Women's Center
San Antonio Stars
San Antonio Society of Women CPAs
San Antonio Women's Chamber of Commerce
San Antonio Women's Hall of Fame
Sistas in Business, Inc.
South Texas Women's Business Center
Susan G. Komen Breast Cancer Foundation
Texas Business Women – Corpus Christi TBW, Mexican American TBW; TBW of San Antonio Texas Nurses Association, District 8
University of Texas at San Antonio Archives
WELEAD
WINGS
Woman at the Well House
Women of AT&T
Women's Faculty Association
Women's Global Connection
Women's Pavilion at HemisFair Park, Inc.
Women's Sports Foundation
Women's Studies Institute - UTSA
Young Women's Christian Association
Zonta Club of San Antonio

Each community is unique and will likely have the same and different organizations. For example, while living in Philadelphia, I was a member of Soroptimists, an international women's organization. The group is not listed with *Can We Talk, SA*. *Can We Talk* was formed more than 30 years ago in San Antonio, Texas. If you are interested in starting a local chapter in your community, email *Can We Talk, USA* in Jacksonville, Florida at CanWeTalkJAX@gmail.com

REFERENCES

[i] Horoho takes oath as first nurse, female surgeon general. Retrieved Nov. 15, 2016 from https://www.army.mil/article/70556/

[ii] Bass, B.M. (2001). Cognitive, social, and emotional intelligence of transformational leaders. In R.E. Riggio, S.E. Murphy, and F.J. Priozzolo (Eds), Multiple Intelligences and Leadership, (pp. 54-77). Mahwah, NJ: Lawrence Earlbaum and Associates.

[iii] Mumford, M.D., Friedrich, T.L., Caughron, J.J., & Byrne, C.L. (2007). Leader cognition in real-world settings: How do leaders think about crises?. The Leadership Quarterly, 18(6), 515-543. doi: 10.1016/j.leaqua.2007.09.002

[iv] Northouse, P. (2012). Leadership: Theory and practice. (6 ed.). Thousand Oaks, California: Sage Publishing.

[v] Northouse, P. (2004)

[vi] New York, Feb. 23 – Mar 8, 2015. Super-Intelligence

[vii] Ibid.

[viii] Wren, J. (1995). The leader's companion: Insights on leadership through the ages. New York, NY: Free Press.

[ix] Reiss, S. (2002). Who am I? The 16 Basic Desires that Motivate our Actions and Define our Personalities. New York, NY: Berkley Publishing Group.

[x] http://powherful.org/

[xi] https://en.wikipedia.org/wiki/Jiddu_Krishnamurti

[xii] Hall, Liz (13 Nov. 2013) Ten tips for being a mindful coach. The International Coach Federation Blog. Retrieved March 20, 2017 from https://coachfederation.org/blog/index.php/1623/

[xiii] Koltko-Rivera, M. E. (2006). Rediscovering the later version of Maslow's Hierarchy of Needs: Self-Transcendence and opportunities for theory, research, and unification. Retrieved from http://academic.udayton.edu/jackbauer/Readings%20595/Koltko-Rivera%202006%20trans%20self-act%20copy.pdf

[xiv] Ibid.

[xv] Rath (2007) StrengthsFinder 2.0. Gallup.

[xvi] Northouse (2004). Leadership: Theory and practice. (6 ed.). Thousand Oaks, California: Sage Publishing.

[xvii] Ibid.

[xviii] http://www.outofservice.com/bigfive/

[xix] http://similarminds.com/cattell-16-factor.html

[xx] http://www.bbc.com/news/magazine-21799703

[xxi] https://tribecafilminstitute.org/films/detail/the_war_to_be_her

[xxii] http://www.cnn.com/videos/tv/2016/05/14/exp-gps-toorpakai-waziristan-squash.cnn

[xxiii] http://www.susansontag.com/SusanSontag/index.shtml

[xxiv] www.aauw.org

[xxv] Hargrove, Masterful Coaching, 1995, p. 15

[xxvi] "Everyone needs a coach" Bill Gates & Eric Schmidt. TED.com. https://www.youtube.com/watch?v=XLF90uwII1k

www.ingramcontent.com/pod-product-compliance
Lightning Source LLC
Chambersburg PA
CBHW021117300426
44113CB00006B/177